The African Running Revolution

Edited by

Dave Prokop

Published by

World Publications

RUNNER'S BOOKLET SERIES NO. 47
May, 1975

Library of Congress Catalog Card Number: 75-282
ISBN – 0-89037-058-3

World Publications, Box 366, Mountain View, CA 94040

Contents

Cover photo: Ben Jipcho, by Steve Sutton/Duomo.

Foreword

I don't know the author's name (his article appeared without a byline), but I vividly remember reading the lines he wrote shortly after the Rome Olympics in 1960. Commenting on Abebe Bikila's marathon victory, he had said, "Abebe's gold medal undoubtedly marks a significant step forward by the vast sporting choir of Africa whose collective voice may rise to a bellow in future Olympic Games. Remember, Africans took the first two places in the Rome marathon (Morocco's Abdesselem Rhadi was second), and four of them were in the first eight (Ethiopia's Abebe Wakgira, seventh; Morocco's Benaisa Bakir, eighth). The world may shortly be astonished at what can happen when African agility and strength are harnessed to scientific training methods."

How remarkably prophetic those words turned out to be! Only a few years later African runners were dominating the distance events at such major international competitions as the '66 Commonwealth Games and the '68 Olympic Games at high-altitude Mexico City. An amazed and admiring sports public marvelled at the success of these athletes as well as their unique approach to running. As Geoff Fenwick, one of the contributors to this book, wrote recently: "The African athletes have brought to the sport refreshing, exciting competitive elements which delight by virtue of their sheer exuberance . . . The uninhibited running of Wilson Kiprugut, Kipchoge Keino (especially in the 1500 meters at Mexico City), Amos Biwott and Filbert Bayi are spendid examples of this approach."

The African Running Revolution is the most complete and incisive book yet published on the phenomenal African success story in track. Written for the most part by men who have been actively involved in the sport in Africa, the book covers a wide range of topics, including the one probably uppermost in the minds of track enthusiasts: what accounts for the tremendous success of these runners? Is a life at altitude the answer (as so many believe)? In his article "Science on the Altitude Factor", altitude-training expert Dr. Jack Daniels of the University of Texas explains what scientific research has to say on the matter.

A telling argument against the "altitude-advantage" theory is that East Africans, of course, are not the only people in the world who live at altitude. Yet only they, among the world's high-altitude dwellers, have collectively made a mark in the track world. In his superb article "In Search of an Explanation", John Manners offers a number of possible anthropological and cultural explanations for the success of these runners.

Athletics, of course, means people. The concluding, and longest, chapter in the book features articles on some of the greatest runners Africa has produced. Included in this chapter is the most complete story yet written on Tanzanian super-runner Filbert Bayi. The author, Tom Sturak, was with Bayi off and on for a week in researching the story.

Whatever your involvement or interest in running, we're sure you'll find *The African Running Revolution* fascinating reading.

– Dave Prokop

Chapter One

A Coach's Viewpoint

by Bob Hancock

Before returning to his native England in 1974, Bob Hancock taught and coached for eight years in Kenya where he earned the reputation of being possibly the most knowledgeable, and certainly one of the most successful, coaches in the country. Among the athletes he has coached are Robert Ouko, Paul Mose and Patrick Onyango (East African record holder in the triple jump: 53'6"). An indication of the esteem in which Hancock is held in Kenya is that he was the only foreigner on the coaching staff of Kenya's '72 Olympic team (he was named to the staff, apparently, on the insistence of the athletes).

While coaching in Kenya, Hancock, who is a former athlete himself, had a day-to-day opportunity to observe first-hand the Kenyan approach to running. As he reports here, the experience led him to re-think his own coaching ideas and convinced him that the African runners, in their uninhibited, natural approach, have much to teach coaches, and therefore athletes, in the more established track nations of the world.

Looking back over Kenya's glorious years of athletics and ahead to the unknown '70s and beyond, one might easily be tempted into thinking that the best days are behind and that Kenya's present crop of young athletes cannot possibly match the achievements of the past. One might well see Ben Jipcho and Kip Keino in a class of super-athlete the likes of which appear only once in a generation from a population the size of Kenya's. You could also argue that the country has been a trifle lucky, for a variety of reasons, in recent international games, and that the medal charts have been unduly flattering to Kenya's athletes.

But those who have visited Kenya and seen at close quarters the simple structure of the sport there will have noticed also the abundance of talent waiting in the wings for its time to arrive. All over the country youngsters are eager to be a part of the track scene, knowing only too well the roles played by their own local heroes. Up and down the land raw talent is rife. And it would be no exaggeration to say that, as yet, we have only seen the tip of the iceberg, as it were.

I first went to Kenya in 1966 and spent some eight years teaching and coaching in two secondary schools in the highlands. During that time a number of outstanding athletes passed through both of these schools, some of them winning medals at Olympic and Commonwealth Games. Perhaps of more significance was the experience of having seen scores of beginners enjoy instant success in athletics but not getting hooked on it. Strangely enough in Kenya, it is only the successful athletes who come back for more. A chap who is fourth or fifth considers himself a flop regardless of the company in which he competes. Winning is so important.

But it's from seeing the average student "have a go" that you realize the base of the pyramid in Kenya is potentially so wide. The fact that the athletic population is still so small is a consequence of a number of social and economic factors—such as there being only one track and field club in all of Kenya at present outside of the schools, colleges and the National Services.

Having participated in track and field a good deal myself before arriving in Kenya, I was immediately struck by the apparent casual approach of the local athlete to his event. Gone were the long, nervous warmups and pre-race tensions of the European. Instead, you would find athletes on the line actually smiling, always with a word for one another, and generally relaxed. As a coach I was, at first, keen to try some of the well-established methods of back home on my own squad of athletes. A good quantity of mileage, plenty of real quality work on the track, and regular use of the stopwatch were the thoughts that came to mind.

"One must always be prepared to learn" is certainly good advice for life, and it wasn't long before I was re-thinking my own coaching ideas in the light of local circumstances. Soon I abandoned the clinical "white" (European) approach to the sport and started toying with a few African ideas.

Since its 19th century revival, track and field has been dominated by the Europeans and Americans. So it's not strange that coaches all over the world have looked to the West for the latest edicts. I am firmly of the opinion that the African athletes, through their achievements in recent years, have much to teach the more established nations of track and field. Perhaps the time has come for European coaches, and those in the other parts of the Western world, to take a big step back and re-examine their own priorities. Will physiologists continue to point the way or can we look at the running events from a different angle, gleaning new information of a non-scientific nature that may prove more effective?

The 400 meters has always been of particular interest to me and in this event particularly African athletes have, I think, generally shown that they can master many of the running problems which European coaches have found necessary to dissect. "Sub-maximal contractions," "the anaerobic state" and "splits" are just some of the terms without which the Africans have managed to do quite well. Can I suggest, in looking at the running events generally, that Filbert Bayi's courageous front-running, Ben Jipcho's strength and competitive flair, and Julius Sang's relaxation and ease of movement are all non-technical approaches which we might loosely tag as African. I am sure that all three have tried to develop their own instinctive approach to running rather than adopt methods through advice they may have received along physiological lines.

All the great 400-meter runners of Africa have displayed an uninhibited approach to their event. Daniel Rudisha saw the event in terms of rhythms. He would describe a race using such expressions as "tick-tick-tick-tick." This was supposed to represent the stride rhythm. If at any stage of the race there had been a need for acceleration, he might later have described this with an increased tempo of his "ticks." He might say, "Tick-tick-tick-tick-tick, and I passed him." Rudisha was no world beater, but he had a great understanding of the event in terms of these rhythms. He once dreamt, he said, of breaking the world record after having been paced all the way by Lee Evans, but coming through at the end by dint of superior rhythm control.

I would venture to suggest that Julius Sang's fundamental approach to the event is to stay relaxed for as long as possible, and to treat his run-in as a sprint, as best he can. His ideal 400 would be to run the full distance on his toes (as he did at Munich), having to contest the last 30 or so meters, and winning through his greater relaxation. The ability to relax is certainly a feature of Kenyan track, the big win often being accompanied by a big grin!

Charles Asati had a different attitude to the event and possessed the comparatively rare characteristic of being able to "turn on" and "turn off." One moment he would be chatting and clowning around, the next he would be producing one of those scintillating 46ers we've seen so many times in Kenya. Well equipped for the event through his basic speed (he's run 20.5 for 200 meters), he tackles the race as an extended sprint, with a natural distribution of effort, allowing, of course, something for the latter stages of the race.

A similar treatment of the event was offered by Hezekiah Nyamau, but being limited in basic speed he had to make the most of the event in his one and only gear. Somehow he would appear to be in the same condition after 50 meters as he would after 350 meters. If you had attempted to ask him about the fundamental problem of lactic acid buildup, he might have shrugged his shoulders and re-engaged you in a conversation about the weather.

All four athletes* I have mentioned exhibited a natural as opposed to a scientific approach to running. But do not equate this to any lack of under-

---

*Editor: Daniel Rudisha was the first Kenyan 400-meter runner to catch the attention of the track world when he missed a bronze medal in the '66 Commonwealth Games on a photo finish. His time of 46.5, in only his sixth race ever over the one-lap distance, was the first real indication of Kenya's vast potential in the event. Charles Asati won the gold medal in the 400 meters (45.0) and a bronze medal in the 200 meters at the '70 Commonwealth Games. Hezekiah Nyamau was a member of Kenya's 4 x 400-meter relay team, along with Asati and Rudisha, that won the silver medal in Mexico City, and a member of the Kenyan team, with Asati and Sang, that won the gold medal in the '72 Olympics in Munich. Sang, of course, was Kenya's 400-meter star at Munich, winning a bronze medal in the 400 and anchoring the 4 x 400 team to victory (in the absence of the US team) with a brilliant 43.5 leg—second fastest in history.

standing of the event on their part. They all have, or had, a great feeling for the event, possibly something they could not express in words, let alone in physiological terms. The African athlete sees his event as a *race*, and not as a series of situations which require his trained response.

These remarks refer exclusively to the one-lap event. But if you were to put distance running under the microscope you would expose a kaleidoscope of varying "natural" ideas and attitudes presented by Africans. However, since my own experience relates only to Kenya, perhaps I'm not entitled to generalize so freely on all African distance runners.

One other area of running where I think Africans excel is in their ability to learn from experience and each other. While you may be thinking of the many occasions on which Kipchoge Keino was beaten on the run-in, I can recall the many coaching situations in which an active athlete, possibly a local champion, might be asked to demonstrate a point—with outstanding results. A hundred well-chosen words on my part could not match the local man's demonstration.

Often one athlete might attach himself to another, usually better, athlete, hoping to learn by copying. African athletes feel a far greater responsibility to each other than European athletes do; there are fewer track "loners," and athletes in a group usually try to help each other rather than the opposite.

When it comes to exchanging ideas, Africans have found certain aspects of the "white" approach to training suitable to their needs. Although I raised some questions earlier about the established methods of training (high mileage, interval training, use of the stopwatch), interval training does occasionally form part of the buildup for many Kenyan runners. I remember helping Ben Jipcho through a training session in Munich prior to the Olympic Games of 1972. He did four half-miles, each under two minutes with about three minutes recovery in between. It was his second workout of the day and he was pleased with the result. The times themselves served their purpose, but they weren't the prime objective of the exercise. Ben was merely checking his form and as he regarded himself as warming down, rather than building up, for the big races ahead, he was quite satisfied.

From my own experience, however, Kenyan athletes do not easily adapt to the discipline that interval running demands. Rather they would prefer to spend a session way off the beaten track on a steep hill, developing racing aggression and generally running to exhaustion.

Apart from my reference to Big Ben above, you'll notice that I have not referred to times or interval distances, which we sometimes consider to be such a vital part of our sport. It is one very happy reflection that you could still have a very enjoyable track meet in Kenya without the use of stopwatch and measuring tape. And perhaps it is this basic understanding that the sport is nothing but a "man versus man" struggle that has put Kenya on the athletics map of the world.

An Elan, a Zest and a Grace

by David Lewis

Welsh-born, Cambridge-educated David Lewis taught in Kenya for several years. While there, he was not only a close observer of the Kenyan athletic scene but also coached Ben Jipcho through the early, formative years of his running career. Lewis is now a journalist in New Zealand.

In the far off days when, as a lad, I used to pack in among the thousands on the terraces of the White City in London to watch the European track gods of the '50s, the black African runners were regarded as a bit of a joke. Particularly in the middle and long distance events, where such quintessentially "British" traits as discipline, strength of character, foresight and reserve were at a premium, the ebullient front-running of the Africans seemed clearly ridiculous.

It should be remembered that of the major spectator sports of that time, when the great British Empire was planting flags on the top of Everest and desperately trying to go out with a bang rather than a whimper, none was more firmly "British," nor more tightly clasped in the grip of the gentlemanly amateur establishment than athletics, or "track and field," as the somewhat less refined Americans insisted on calling it. Administered, controlled and disciplined internationally by the immaculately tailored ranks of the landed and financial aristocracy, the sport in Britain, its dominions and colonies cherished ideals harking back to the good old days pre-Coubertin, when everyone knew his place in the divine scheme of things.

As if to prove how eternally proper was this best of all possible worlds, there appeared in 1954 a living, breathing incarnation of all that centuries of imperial travail had stood for—all decked out in athletic gear and running spikes. Arising like a blond, Aryan vision from the mists of Oxfordshire, Roger Bannister stepped onto the Oxford University Iffley Road track with some gentlemen companions and shortly afterwards offered the first four-minute mile for Elizabeth, England and St. George.

Dr. Roger Bannister, brave, self-effacing, dedicated (but not unbearably so), a gentleman, a scholar, an amateur, handsome, intelligent, articulate and talented, dashing off the odd world record in between preparations for a lifetime devoted to alleviating human suffering—now there was a hero for you, fans, one to awe the ghastly rabble-rousers out there in the colonies stirring up trouble.

Bannister and chums were gracious proof, to all who wanted to believe it, of the one great truth which supposedly lay behind the achievements of the Empire. No matter how daunting the obstacles, how determined the opposition, how difficult the path, etc., etc., there was nothing that could not be achieved by a gentleman, provided he was British, an amateur and white.

In those days it was hardly surprising that the African athlete was a figure of fun rather than admiration. In Kenya, the British way of doing things had been imitated to the letter in external appearances for over 60 years. A few optimists had even founded a body known as the Kenya Amateur Athletic Association in the early '50s, but there were no facilities worth mentioning, next to no coaches, and only intermittent encouragement was given local athletes. But, of course, this was to be expected since, by colonial definition, the sporting hero was affluent, articulate, priviledged and white. It was pointless, therefore, to urge an African peasant to aspire to athletic performances of heroic stature.

When, every now and again, some benevolent colonial administrator recommended that one of his boys be shipped out to run around a real European track made of cinders, spectators knew full well what to expect of the lad. And he seldom let them down. He would line up at the start of a middle or long distance race and when the gun went off, more often than not, he would bolt like a jackrabbit down the track, opening up a gap of 30 or 40 yards over his more "serious" white rivals. They usually left him to it, secure in the knowledge that he would only last a couple of laps before dropping back and disappearing into the rear of the field. Eventually he would be lapped, and often, looking cold and unhappy and a long way from home, he would drop out. The African was the clown at the court of the European athlete in the days when only a handful of nations produced world-class performers. He was a temporary diversion amid the grim business of setting records and establishing new standards.

THEY HAVE LONG STOPPED LAUGHING

But somehow, just a dozen years after Dr. Bannister set that most celebrated of all athletic records, the African athlete was no longer a clown. A bewildered Western public watched the jester usurp the throne of their gentleman amateur princes, and they stopped laughing at him.

The emergence of the African athlete reflected much broader social and political phenomena, as the values which Dr. Bannister personified in the early '50s—amateurism, priviledge and white imperialism—were gradually being replaced by something more in tune with a world which is independent, predominantly impoverished and predominantly colored. It was as if, having decided that his newly acquired political independence also meant sporting independence, the African athlete in the '60s stepped across the arid wasteland of colonial thinking and arrogant British values. A proud procession of black distance runners marched into the holy places where the white man celebrated his sporting rites, invaded them and took up residence there with a grace and charm that astounded those who had grown accustomed to thinking of the African runner as the fool up front who would soon run out of puff.

Ironically, the graceful and charming African champions of today still have more in common with the "clowns" of 20 years ago than they do with their contemporary Western rivals. Of course, the modern African runner is better conditioned and a more canny competitor than his predecessors, but his joyous exuberence in a race contrasts just as sharply with the seriousness of the whites running with him as it did back in the '50s.

That so many African athletes have retained such an apparently carefree approach to their sport amid the rigors of the highest level of international competition mystifies most Western observers. In the case of the Kenyans, who as a national group have been by far the continent's most successful athletes, altitude is certainly a major factor in their success and easy-going ways. Every one of the great Kenyan runners of the past decade comes from a high-altitude area and is the product of generations born and bred up in the mountains. This probably goes a long way towards explaining their extraordinary natural gifts; it also helps explain the apparently light training which the Kenyan stars seem to put in compared to their European counterparts.

The Kenyan athlete has been running and walking huge distances since he could stand. By contrast, even the most underprivileged European's upbringing might appear rather pampered. By the time he is a mature athlete, the Kenyan has had a backlog of massive endurance work and a super-abundance of mileage, plus his birthright, immense lung capacity—the product of generations who have lived in the thin air of the mountains. Conditioned to run at high altitude and thus capable of resisting the effects of oxygen debt until very late in a race, the Kenyan can descend to sea level and bring to bear often unassailable advantages over his naturally weaker European rival.

The sea-level athlete, meanwhile, has recourse only to super doses of mileage to counter this. The 150-200-mile-a-week runner, or the Lydiard marathon man, is, in fact, attempting, at the outer limits of his endurance, to buy back 20 or so years of relatively soft Western upbringing, in order to rid himself of his low-altitude background so that he may put himself on something near level terms.

THE MYTH OF SUPPOSED LACK OF TRAINING

Hence, the myth of the Kenyan's supposed lack of training. The Kenyan has, in fact, been training solidly every day of his life since he was parked in the corner of his mother's mud and wattle hut as a baby and encouraged to survive. His lifetime's training will have built up an incredible physical toughness, a resilience under stress and an astonishingly high tolerance of pain. Two hundred miles a week, even if it were feasible at high altitude, would be an exercise in pointless boredom to the Kenyan athlete. The often-asked question posed by the bewildered European observer, "What on earth could they do if they trained?" is, therefore, ill-informed.

To the Kenyan, 40-50 miles a week on average is quite sufficient, done at altitude and rounded off when sharpening time comes around with some tough hill work and a time trial or two. Even better is to do the 40-50 miles in races, as can be done during the very popular cross-country season. In any case, the Kenyan is probably singularly fortunate he does not need to put in his 150 weekly miles, in view of the colossal psychological and physical stress problems modern training mileages are causing their practitioners.

Thus, in part because of his altitude background, when the Kenyan appears at an international arena, he seems, compared to his European rivals, fresh and eager to run. His enthusiam has not been drained away over mile after mile of road or track, and he is not burdened with the anxiety bred of interminable hours invested in training.

Perhaps an equally important factor in the Kenyan athlete's seemingly relaxed approach to his sport is the system he comes from—a wide-open, low-pressure national athletic structure which grew up in the '60s and which channeled the enormous emerging talent.

The system, which is sometimes accidentally, sometimes deliberately a unique blend of the amateur enthusiast and the professional government administrator, still has many faults. It is appallingly short of money, facilities and equipment. It struggles hard to make progress in the complex technicalities of field events, sometimes achieves a little but soon sinks back to where it started in the face of ever-increasing world standards. It has, in spite of a few determined efforts, still failed to provide for women athletes the opportunities for success it offers its male stars. The woman athlete is still regarded as a freak, taking a little time off before returning promptly to her age-old child-bearing, water-carrying, dowry-attracting, husband-obeying traditional role.

Nevertheless, for all its faults and lapses, the system has produced numerous superb athletes in the relatively short period since Kenyan independence, and it has done so without subjecting the athletes to such pressures that the enjoyment they so clearly get out of their effort is diminished.

Perhaps the Kenyans are the true amateurs of today, participating for the love of the sport. It is tempting to suggest that, after all, they do have things in common with Dr. Bannister and the four-minute milers. Tempting, but mistaken, for although there may have been some basic human truths hidden away in the murky imperial message, they have been so distorted and misused that they can no longer be truthfully represented by a contemporary white sporting hero.

AN INTANGIBLE QUALITY

The unique quality of the Kenyan athletes is really intangible, outside the realm of foreign analysis, something truly Kenyan. How else does one explain the catalogue of graces the Kenyans have brought to athletics: the easy floating, relaxed rhythm of Sang: the careless, offhand brilliance of Asati; the unfailing courtesy of a visiting Kenyan squad; the old world manners and gentle friendship of Richard Juma; the humility of Temu; the keen analytical sense of Koskei and Ndoo; the humane dignity of Jipcho; the unfailing gentleman that is the great Keino; the sheer enjoyment of every aspect of the sport endlessly communicated by an international team of Kenyans? It is a zest for living, an elan and grace, an affirmation, which needs no ponderous verbal expression, of the joys of physical achievement.

And it is pride. A pride that comes from the instinctive knowledge that although the whites may have invented the game of track and field, the success the Kenyans have made of playing it is due to something over which the white man had no control and will never understand— something passed on from generation to generation, intensely African and visible for a while in all its glory in such a simple activity as track running.

In the final analysis, one is left with the conclusion that instead of spending our time seeking explanations for the Kenyan phenomenon, we should perhaps be seeking explanations as to why we in the West have made of a joyous expression of physical performance such a complicated, stress-ridden, expensive, pressurized mirror to our own frustrated society.

The Kenyans, and the other African runners, have revitalized the sport. It will be very interesting to observe whether the years ahead will see the lessons they offer learned or whether, as is unfortunately all too likely, they will be seduced by the sophistication of the alternative approach offered by the more experienced nations.

Chapter Two

History, Tradition in African Track
by Geoff Fenwick

Geoff Fenwick lived in Africa for many years and is an expert on African athletics. A long-time contributor to Runner's World magazine, he now lives in his native England.

Africa's track heritage is rich. It is a continent in which travel by foot is traditional. Over the centuries there have been camels and, in certain places, horses to carry the lucky few, but for the majority of people travel was, and still is, walking or running. This is accepted even in developed areas. Often walking is the alternative to waiting for tomorrow's bus—and this assumes that one lives near a bus stop! Even if one does, tropical weather conditions often preclude motorized travel.

If one is lucky enough to own a car in Africa it is possible to encounter pastoralists prodding their gaunt cattle along in the dawn light and, on one's return journey, to pass these same people in the late evening 30 or 40 miles farther on. Such journeys on foot, through the dust, storms and heat of the tropical day, are not uncommon in Africa.

These traditions are not, however, easily converted into formal competition, and athletic development throughout the continent has certainly not been uniform. The first organized running competitions probably occurred in South Africa where a settled white population living in an agreeable climate created a club structure based on the western European model, except that the membership was open only to white people. Success in marathon events by white South Africans in the early Olympic Games encouraged an interest in road running which is still very strong. There are more road races promoted annually in South Africa than there are in the rest of the African countries put together. And it is

probably fair to say that Africa's best known race is the Comrades Marathon, a 54-mile-long event held annually between the cities of Durban and Pietermaritz-burg.

Probably because of an early start plus an excellent climate and good facilities, South Africa has produced at one time or another hurdlers, sprinters and distance runners of international caliber. If the output is smaller now, the main reason probably lies in the fact that South Africa's policy of apartheid has denied her athletes the international competition essential for development at the highest level.

In the rest of the continent sporting traditions vary immensely. Some countries have little recorded evidence of sporting activities. Rwanda, Burundi, Somalia, Zaire and the Sudan have produced no athletes of note. Generally, the former colonies of France and Great Britain are likely to have some athletics tradition and thus the strongest countries in athletics are Nigeria, Ghana, the Ivory Coast and Senegal in the west; Kenya, Ethiopia, Uganda and Tanzania in the east; and Tunisia, Algeria and Morocco in the north. Of these, only Ethiopia has not been colonized by Great Britain or France.

To cite an example, Uganda formed a track and field association in 1925. Nine years later saw the inaugural East African Championships, initially between Kenya and Uganda. Tanzania joined in this competition in 1955, and Ethiopia and Zambia have also been entering teams in recent years. These championships, possibly the first international series between African nations, have, without a doubt, been instrumental in the great improvement of track performances in East Africa.

It was many years, however, before African countries made their mark in events outside the continent. For a long time their athletes represented the colonial nations. As long ago as 1928, El Ouafi represented France in the Olympics and won the marathon event. El Ouafi was Algerian by birth. French cross-country teams had their sprinkling of North Africans for many years. One of these runners was the great Alain Mimoun, another Algerian, who won silver medals behind Emil Zatopek at the 1948 and 1952 Olympics. Mimoun finally triumphed over Zatopek in the 1956 Olympic marathon, in which he won the gold medal. Now a coach, Mimoun is still active as a veteran runner in France. Other African athletes who successfully represented France in European and Olympic championships include El Mabrouk (1500 meters) and Papa Gallo (high jump).

Great Britain tended to make use of her West Indian colonies in a similar way. But a number of African athletes who came to Britain to study represented that country in championship events also, probably because they would not have been able to participate in such high level competition in any other way. Most of these athletes were long and triple jumpers from West Africa. Among them were S.O. Williams, K. Olowu and Prince Adedoyin.

During the 1950s some progress was made in African athletics, and national teams began to tour Europe. A Nigerian team, for example, toured Great Britain in 1950. Gradually, African nations began to compete in international

Scenes like this were typical at the '68 Olympics in Mexico City, where Africans won every race from 1500 meters up. Here Ethiopia's Fikru Diguefu leads midway through the 10,000 meters. Africans swept the medals in the race. (Horst Muller)

events in their own right. For those countries which were still British colonies, there was one great advantage: they could take part in the Commonwealth Games. Success, albeit of a minor sort, came quite swiftly. In the 1954 Commonwealth Games, E.A. Ifeajuna of Nigeria won a gold medal and Patrick Etolu of Uganda a silver medal in the high jump. On the track, progress was slower. It was 1962 before an African representative, Serafino Antao of Kenya, won a gold medal. And Antao, being a Goan (of Indian origin) domiciled in East Africa, was not, in the strictest sense of the word, African.

At Olympic level, the first successes came in 1960. Abebe Bikila (Ethiopia) and Abdesselem Rhadi (Morocco) took the first two places in the marathon and Nyandika Maiyoro of Kenya came seventh in the 5000 meters. Further triumphs came in the 1964 Olympics in the person of the remarkable Bikila in the marathon and, to a lesser extent, Mohamed Gammoudi of Tunisia in the 10,000 meters (a silver medal) and Wilson Kiprugut of Kenya in the 800 meters (a bronze, giving Kenya her first ever Olympic medal). Also in those Games, Mamo Wolde of Ethiopia finished fourth in the 10,000 and Kipchoge Keino fifth in the 5000. Of course, Keino's performances the following year—two world records (in the 3000 and 5000), and a brilliant series of races against Ron Clarke and Michel Jazy in Scandinavia— was to focus world attention on Kenyan running for the first time. The real African breakthrough, however, came in the 1966 Commonwealth Games in Kingston, Jamaica, where Keino won two events and Naftali Temu scored a stunning upset victory over Clarke in the six-mile, and in the 1968 Olympic Games in Mexico City, where African runners won every event from 1500 meters up (Keino, 1500; Gammoudi, 5000; Temu, 10,000; Wolde, marathon; and Kenya's youthful Amos Biwott, the steeplechase). Since then, African triumphs have become virtually taken for granted and names such as Keino, Jipcho, Akii-Bua and Bayi are known throughout the world. In addition, there are now continental championships in the form of the African Games, although this competition is held somewhat irregularly.

It would be unjust not to mention some of the fine athletes who, unheralded and unknown outside their native countries, ploughed lonely but important furrows in the early days when Africans were struggling to make an impression on the sporting world.

There were Nyandika Maiyoro and Arere Anentia, the fathers of Kenyan distance running in the 1950s. It was such men who provided the inspiration for future Olympic gold medallists like Keino and Naftali Temu. Temu, never a consistent performer, is almost forgotten now despite his gold medals in the '66 Commonwealth Games and the '68 Olympic Games. Wilson Kiprugut, a fearsome competitor, won silver and bronze medals at 800 meters in two Olympic Games, yet his efforts have become submerged in the high tide of more recent Kenyan successes.

If these men are almost forgotten, then two other East African runners were never sufficiently well known to be remembered. Neither Pascal Myfiomi nor John Stephen were consistent enough to be outstandingly successful but in

Athletes like Kenya's Fatwell Kimaiyo are proof that East Africa doesn't produce distance runners and steeplechasers only. Kimaiyo won the 110-meter high hurdles, in 13.7, at the '74 Commonwealth Games and ran 49.6 to finish fourth in the 400-meter hurdles. (Mark Shearman)

their day they were among the best in East Africa. In 1963, for example, My-fiomi destroyed the best of the Kenyans over six miles, and in 1970, Stephen ran 2:15:05 to place fifth in the Commonwealth Games marathon. Myfiomi and Stephen were Tanzania's first runners of class and without their example and inspiration, Filbert Bayi might never have become the great runner that he is.

Uganda's distance men have never achieved their true potential. Uganda's best man to date has probably been Robert Rwakojo, who made the mile final in the Commonwealth Games at Kingston, Jamaica in 1966. Uganda has, how-ever, a fine hurdling tradition. This began in the late '50s. Jean Baptiste Okello reached the semi-finals of the high hurdles in the Rome Olympics in 1960 and missed the final by an eyelash. Two years later Benson Ishiepai won a bronze medal in the 400-meter hurdles at the Commonwealth Games. The tradition was continued when transplanted Kenyan Bill Koskei won a silver medal in the 1970 Commonwealth Games and came to fruition with Akii-Bua's superb Olympic victory in Munich. Okello, Ishiepai, Koskei and Akii-Bua have been hurdlers of a caliber rarely produced outside Europe or the United States. Few countries have produced four such men in a decade and a half.

Another highly talented erstwhile champion of Uganda was Jorem Ochana who never won anything more important than the East African championship in the 400-meter hurdles. Ochana had perhaps as much talent as Akii-Bua but he lacked the personality to succeed at the highest level. Okello never achieved the success he deserved for another reason: he fell and broke his leg while thatching a roof shortly after the Rome Olympics.

Add to the Ugandans such Kenyan hurdlers as Bartonjo Rotich, Kimaru Songok and Kipkemboi Yego, all Commonwealth Games medallists in the 400-meter hurdles (in '58, '62 and '70 respectively), and Fatwell Kamaiyo, winner of the 110-meter high hurdles at the '74 Commonwealth Games, and it's clear that East Africa doesn't produce distance men and steeplechasers only.

Mention should also be made of the considerable number of African 400-meter runners who made an impact at international level in the '60s. They include Amos Omolo of Uganda, Claver Kamanya of Tanzania, Amadou Gakou of Sene-gal, Tenegne Bezabeh of Ethiopia, Samuel Bugri of Ghana, plus the Kenyans Charles Asati, Hezekiah Nyamau, Naftali Bon, Daniel Rudisha and Julius Sang. All of these men have reached an Olympic semi-final at least. Many of them have won medals. This area of African success is fascinating, for no one can claim that high altitude favors the preparation of 400-meter runners. Furthermore, many of these men did not come from high-altitude countries.

The documentation of athletics tends to be slight in Africa. Past perfor-mances are quickly forgotten, especially when there are superlative runners such as Filbert Bayi and Ben Jipcho on the scene. Nevertheless, the athletes mentioned in the last few paragraphs all played an important part in converting Africa's heri-tage and tradition into the hard currency of international success.

Clearly, Africa brims with running talent. But there is no room for compla-cency. In many African countries the number of top-class athletes is very small. European countries have come and gone as track powers. One thinks of Swe-den, Hungary and Finland in this respect, although Finland has staged a recovery. If some African countries are not to meet the same fate, the natural talents of their athletes will have to be backed up with more assistance and better facilities.

The Talent Distribution
by Geoff Fenwick

If success at international level is taken as a criterion, then the distribution of athletic talent in Africa is markedly geographical. Some countries appear to produce sprinters, hurdlers and jumpers, while others develop long distance runners. In some areas, field events are highly developed. In a number of countries, track and field as a sport hardly exists at all.

Four factors seem to contribute to this geographical distribution: temperature, altitude, historical background and the availability of facilities. When these factors are examined one by one, the reasons for the distribution rapidly become much clearer.

TEMPERATURE

Most of the African continent is warm throughout the year and thus daily outdoor training is possible. Tropical temperatures are quite favorable for hurdlers, sprinters and jumpers, and, given the right historical background and facilities, such athletes are found in most parts of the continent. The exception is the north, where dry regions of sand and stone predominate, making it unlikely that sprinters, hurdlers and jumpers will occur in sufficient numbers to ensure a reasonable standard of performance.

Obviously, in areas where temperatures are too high, middle and long distance running will be unpopular because racing could be difficult (and even dangerous) and training enervating. Thus few good long-distance runners are found in hot, damp countries such as Ghana, the Ivory Coast or Zaire.

In the north and south of the continent the weather is similar to that in southern Europe, with four definite seasons in the year as opposed to the periods of rain and drought encountered in many countries closer to the Equator. So one finds that Morocco, Tunisia and Algeria in the north and South Africa in the south have all done well in international distance events.

ALTITUDE

Since Abebe Bikila's victory in the Rome Olympics in 1960, it has become obvious that athletes who spend most of their lives at 6000 feet or more have a distinct advantage over athletes living closer to sea level when it comes to long distance running. (*Editor:* Many people believe this and it may be true, but there is no scientific proof that it is—see article on page 40 by University of Texas physiologist Dr. Jack Daniels.) Hence, some tropical countries of the high African tableland which were previously thought to be too close to the Equator for the successful development of middle and long distance runners have, during the last decade, produced runners of the highest caliber.

Of these countries, Kenya and Ethiopia have stood out, of course, but Tanzania and Uganda have developed some fine runners as well. In all four countries, the heat is tempered by the high altitude and hard training is possible.

HISTORICAL BACKGROUND

Many countries in Africa are barren in terms of competitive athletics—for example, Botswana, Malawi, Mozambique, Zaire and Somalia. Yet the people of these countries are not physically inferior to those of Ghana, Nigeria, Senegal or Kenya. What they tend to suffer from is lack of tradition in respect to organized athletics.

As mentioned previously, the African countries which were formerly the colonies of France or Great Britain are likely to have some track and field tradition, and it is from these countries that most of the better athletes come. Even then, some of these former colonies are much better off than others. Track has flourished in Kenya. In Zambia and Malawi progress has been much slower. Yet all are former British colonies. Nevertheless, nations with some tradition tend to be able to make progress much quicker than those where there is no tradition. A huge country like Zaire, for instance, has yet to produce an athlete of note. But then Zaire's former rulers, the Belgians, do not appear to have had the same strong interest in introducing sport to their colonies as did the British and the French.

AVAILABILITY OF FACILITIES

Africa's potential in track and field has only been revealed in the last 10 years. Yet talent, favorable climates and high altitudes are meaningless without decent facilities. Without a track to run on, for instance, a talented middle-distance runner from the slopes of Mount Kenya will never reach his true potential. The facilities factor is crucial to all athletes everywhere but it is probably fair to state that in Africa it determines quite ruthlessly which nations succeed and which do not even begin to produce sportsmen. Why else would such large countries as the Sudan, Zaire and Botswana be so puny in track terms?

The majority of Africans still live in scattered settlements. To succeed in track and field it is usually necessary that young Africans go to live in towns or cities. Otherwise they are unlikely to have the time or the facilities needed to do well. This might explain why the overall standard in a rich country like South Africa is higher than anywhere else, although whether good facilities are available to *all* South Africans is obviously open to doubt, given the country's present policy of apartheid.

With the right talents and the right traditions, Africans are most likely to succeed when they are close to centers where facilities are good. There are a number of examples which seem to illustrate this. Most of them are related to long distance runners at high altitudes but, in a lesser way, they hold good for all African athletes.

There seems, at first glance, little reason for Ethiopia and, to an even greater degree, Kenya being so markedly superior to Uganda and Tanzania (Filbert

The great Abebe Bikila in Tokyo, 1964, when he became the first man ever to win the Olympic marathon a second time. His Tokyo winning time—2:12:11.8—is still the Olympic record. Tragically, an auto accident shortly after the '68 Olympics left Bikila paralyzed from the waist down. On October 25, 1973, at the age of 41, he died of a stroke. (Horst Muller)

Bayi notwithstanding) in middle and long distance running. All four countries possess tableland at high altitude and have facilities which are quite reasonable compared with those of many African countries. All four have experienced the influence of talented coaches, both local and expatriate. The difference might well lie in the fact that in both Ethiopia and Kenya the areas of athletic excellence center on, or are near, the major cities with available facilities. Thus both the cities of Addis Ababa and Nairobi have little difficulty in drawing talented runners from the surrounding districts.

The situation is different in Uganda and Tanzania. In Uganda the areas of high altitude are located in the west, several hundred miles from the capital city of Kampala. Similarly, in Tanzania the capital, Dar es Salaam, is on the coast and a long way from the highland of the interior. Consequently, it is difficult to attract talented athletes in the required numbers to move from their home areas to the centers where the facilities exist.

It might be claimed that Tanzania has solved the problem. Certainly they have one extremely talented runner in the person of Filbert Bayi. One might still ask, however, how many more might have been developed if the capital city had been elsewhere. In fact, the president of Tanzania proposes to move his capital inland so that there will be close contact between his government and the areas where the agricultural reforms, which the government supports, are being instituted. If this move does take place, the face of Tanzanian athletics might well change.

Although this theory might be seen to relate specifically to distance running, it might well apply to other events. In Uganda, policemen and soldiers have traditionally been recruited from the northern tribes whose menfolk are known for their strength and stature. If these tribes were centered on Kampala in the extreme south, Uganda's strength in the field events might well be much greater.

OTHER FACTORS

It is likely that there are other reasons which influence the geographic distribution of Africa's athletes. There is, of course, the factor of wealth. The richer a country is, the more likely it is to expend money on recreation and facilities.

There is also the question of terrain. Countries where rain forest or desert predominate are unlikely to be places where athletics can be promoted.

Yet another factor is concerned with how particular cultures see the role of women within their society. African women are as hardy as their menfolk, but in countries where the Muslim faith predominates their participation in sport is often discouraged. Indeed, it is only in areas where education has emancipated African women from their traditional roles of burden-carrier and laborer that any measure of success has been achieved.

The most fascinating aspect of the African athletic picture is that after so many years of dormancy it has been constantly changing since Bikila's 1960 Olympic success. There is every reason to believe that rapid change will continue. Botswana, for example, is at present a poor, arid country dependent on cattle rearing and subsistence agriculture. Recently found mineral deposits suggest that this state of affairs in the country might soon change. A wealthy Botswana might rival even neighboring South Africa in athletics strength in quite a short time.

The African Approach to Competition
by Geoff Fenwick

"If God wants you to win, then you will win."
—Wilson Kiprugut 1964.

It depends upon where you start. In many of the most primitive African societies, competition is not greatly welcomed. The people of the forests and the the deserts require close cooperation merely to exist. Competition of any sort can be dangerous.

Yet there are many primitive tribes, particularly the pastoral ones, who practice the ultimate in competition. Try to wean them away to more organized, less fatal kinds of sport and you will fail. Running is for capture or escape. Throwing spears is for killing or wounding—whether the target be animals or men.

It is difficult to explain to such a tribesman the purpose of running around an oval track, continually returning to one's starting point. To lure him you need a cow for a prize or perhaps a bicycle. In the event of him winning the latter, he will be much too busy riding it to bother with competitive running again. The pastoralist, for all his talent, has his own preconceived notions concerning the true nature of competition.

More settled people, however, particularly those living near towns and cities, are more interested in pitting their skills against one another in what the hunters and pastoralists of the wide open spaces might regard as somewhat superficial sports.

Soccer, track and field, and boxing are the sports most usually practiced in African countries where there has been much sporting development. Usually one encounters great enthusiasm. One is likely to be joined on evening training runs by friendly, talkative pedestrians who will accompany you until their destination is reached or their way and yours part. There is little of the obloquy which onlookers so often heap on road runners in the Western world.

Competition is usually enthusiastic, particularly in the non-technical events. I cannot recall any mile race that I have watched in Africa where the first lap was not completed in close to 60 seconds.

Athletics clubs in the Western sense are not common in Africa. The economic structure of most countries does not allow for fee-paying clubs open to the general public. Consequently, most athletes are to be found in schools, colleges, universities, armies and police forces.

Attitudes toward competition tend to vary from institution to insitution, but generally prowess in sport is not detrimental to career prospects in military and para-military organizations. Often it can be a positive advantage. Both Abebe Bikila and Kipchoge Keino received considerable promotions during their careers in athletics.

In educational establishments, however, the rewards are not always too obvious. Sporting ability might help to secure a school or college place, providing the athlete has the minimum educational requirements, but it will not keep him there if his academic record is poor. Thus athletes in educational establishments are unlikely to be devoted to sport. And the more advanced the establishment, the more likely this will be. It is easy to be critical of the students in this situation, since many of them certainly have a considerable amount of leisure time. Only when one is aware of the great struggle which most African youths face to secure any sort of formal education is one likely to view the situation with more sympathy.

At regional level the competitive instinct is often high. In Africa regions are often organized on a tribal basis and this tends to reinforce competitive attitudes. I can remember a trio of gaunt cattle drovers winning a team award in the marathon championship of Uganda many years ago. They had not discarded their long black cloaks for the run and they carried their long drovers cattle sticks all of the way. On receiving their awards they brandished their sticks upwards and forward in salute, exclaiming "Lango," which was the region of that hardiest of tribes, the Langi. Beneath their black cloaks they wore the vest of Lango, one of the most exotic athletics vests I have ever seen. Against a pink background was emblazoned the figure of a large black rhino, symbolic of the wild region from which these tough men came.

"ABEBE BIKILA," THE VOICES CALLED

Abebe Bikila's Olympic victory in 1960 provided a great boost to competition at all levels. It meant a great deal to many African people that an unknown black man could so easily defeat the best long distance runners in the world in the hardest race of all. Thereafter, Bikila represented the dreams and hopes of every African boy who ran, even of those who did so only to get to work on time. Often in the early '60s in Africa soft voices would greet a road runner from the wayside as he practiced in the evenings; "Abebe Bikila" the voices would call and they were not a mockery but a reminder that a 1000 miles to the north there lived the greatest long distance runner in the world—and he was African.

At the highest level Bikila's Olympic victory influenced African athletics in two ways. First, it convinced African athletes and their coaches that their own forms of training were not inferior but merely different to those of other places (although Bikila, in fact, was coached by a European resident in Ethiopia, Onni Niskanen of Sweden). Second, it encouraged African runners to forge ahead with their own approach to tactics rather than trying to adopt those of other continents. At first sight crude and unsophisticated, these tactics embodied a natural, non-technical approach to running. The uninhibited running of Wilson Kiprugut, Keino (especially in the 1500 meters at the Mexico Olympics), Amos Biwott and Filbert Bayi are splendid examples of this approach.

No one should think, though, that African athletes are all brawn and no brains. They have their own ideas on how to create psychological advantages and their running is rarely thoughtless. It is ironic that some of their gamesmanship is attributed to competitive naivete when, in fact, they are not above using mild chicanery.

THE ADVANTAGE OF GLORIOUS UNCERTAINTY

There seems little doubt that one factor which contributes to the competitive approach of Africans is the mass media, or rather the lack of it. Television is as yet not highly developed in Africa and newspapers tend to be parochial in content. People are not submerged in the welter of sporting details which television programs bring to some nations. Nor is statistical information readily available. Consequently, whereas athletes in many Western countries are acutely aware of the caliber and performance of their rivals, Africans have not much more than glorious uncertainty. This might be reflected in their uninhibited approach to the the sport and might well eliminate potential neurosis. Many an American or European athlete would welcome the luxury of such ignorance.

Religion also plays its part. A fatalistic view of life is not uncommon in Africa. This applies particularly to people of the Muslim faith, but in general Africans regard meeting the demands of each new day as more important than the delayed gratification of some future goal in the months or years ahead. As Omari, a one-time marathon champion of Uganda, used to say, "If God is willing then you will win." Thus the heart searching and guilt which wracks many a defeated athlete is not notable for its presence among African runners. While they will strive their utmost to carve out their own individual fate in life, they are unlikely to be concerned with post mortems.

This happy-go-lucky philosophy tends to permeate the whole life of many African sportsmen. Often its sheer simplicity forces the stranger to stand back and re-think the values of his own culture. The story of Patrick Etolu illustrates this well.

Patrick was a fine high jumper who rose to international status in the late '50s. At one time he could clear almost seven feet, no inconsiderable feat in those days. As his zest for competition waned he travelled less and less from his home in Teso in the north of Uganda, coming to the occasional national championship when he thought that there was the likelihood of an overseas tour.

Some time after Patrick's self-imposed retirement one of my friends was visiting the Teso district. Playing tennis one day, he noticed that one of the young ball boys was wearing a distinctive blue vest. The ball boy was one of Patrick's sons and he led the visitor to the former champion's modest house. Patrick was pleased to see an old acquaintance and while they talked, his visitor noticed a valuable, ornately decorated ashtray stuffed to the brim with cigarette butts. It was, in fact, a memento given to Patrick in recognition of the time he broke the British Commonwealth high jump record.

"You should keep it for display," the friend urged. "I can send you as many ordinary ashtrays as you want."

"Good," said Patrick, "We can do a swap then."

It took our friend some time to understand the message, perhaps because he had never thought about it in that particular way. But, after all, an ashtray is to put ash in. And if on one day in your life you were fortunate enough to break a record, you have no need to be reminded of the feat.

Chapter Three

In Search of an Explanation
by John Manners

What is the explanation for the phenomenal success story of the East African distance runners? The common answer given is: a life at altitude. But if altitude is indeed the explanation, why is it that of all the people in the world who live at altitude "the only high-altitude dwellers," to quote John Manners, "who collectively have made any mark in the track world come from peoples (i.e., tribes) living in a region that extends from the headwaters of the Blue Nile in the Ethiopian highlands south along the western rim of the Great Rift Valley through western Kenya and eastern Uganda into northern Tanzania"?

And what accounts for the disproportionate success of Kenya's Kalenjin and Kisii tribes, who between them have accounted for all 45 of Kenya's Olympic and Commonwealth Games medals since 1963! (Kenya has more than 30 tribes in all.) In this fascinating, superbly-researched article, Manners offers a number of possible anthropological and cultural explanations for the success of the East Africans in distance running.

John Manners is ideally qualified to write about the East African runners from an anthropological point of view. An American, he spent a year in colonial Kenya as a 12-year-old, accompanying his father, who was doing anthropological research among the Kalenjin. John returned to Kenya for three years (1968-'71) as a Peace Corps volunteer to teach English and coach track at a secondary school in the Kalenjin area. He reported for the BBC African Service at the Munich Olympics and has written on track for the Daily Nation (Nairobi), Track and Field News, Africa Report and Sports Illustrated. He now lives in Baltimore, Md.

While world class athletes in events from the discus to the marathon are scattered almost all over the African continent, when the casual track fan thinks of Africa, chances are he thinks of East African* distance runners—and not without reason. From 1960 to 1972, the period during which most of the continent's 40-odd nations gained their independence, Africans won 28 Olympic medals in track and field. All but one of those medals have been in running events of 400 meters or longer, and all but six have been won by citizens of three countries in eastern Africa: Kenya, Ethiopia and Uganda. The exceptions are a bronze medal in the 200 meters in 1960 by Abdoulaye Seye, a Senegalese running for France, a silver medal in the 1960 marathon by Moroccan Abdesselem Ben Rhadi, and Mohamed Gammoudi's four medals in the 5000 and 10,000 meters at the 1964, '68 and '72 Games. Gammoudi is a Tunisian.

Results of other major international competitions with widespread African participation show an even greater geographical concentration of running success. Of 41 medals won by Africans in men's track events at the last three British Commonwealth Games, 32 were won by East Africans (from Kenya, Uganda and Tanzania), 28 of those by Kenyans. And at the last All-Africa Games in Lagos, Nigeria in 1973, East Africans took 22 of 24 possible medals in individual men's running events from 400 meters up.

Of course, there's nothing unusual about a particular region or country enjoying disproportionate success in a sport. But why are East Africans so good at middle and long distance running? Certainly track can't provide the kind of instant escape from poverty that is commonly supposed to be the incentive that has produced all those Caribbean baseball players and Panamanian jockeys—and to some extent, the disproportionate numbers of American blacks in so many US professional sports. Even with the ITA professional track group on the scene and the availability of scholarships to American colleges, a gifted athlete interested in big money would look to some sport other than track. And East Africa's running successes began long before pro track became a reality or US college scholarships were regularly offered to African athletes.

But there are other incentives, you might say. What about national recognition—as in the case of all those Australian swimmers, or, better yet, the Finnish distance runners? To be sure, East African runners of international caliber get some recognition at home, as they would in any country, and the most successful of them—Bikila, Keino, Jipcho, Akii-Bua and Bayi—are bona fide national heroes in their respective countries. But in none of those countries is track and field anything like the national sport it is in Finland, or even an overwhelming local favorite, as in, say, Eugene, Oregon in the US. On the national level, track and field, or athletics as it's commonly known in East Africa, is at best a distant second in popularity to soccer. None of the four East African governments takes much interest in track except around the time of the Olympics or the Commonwealth Games, and in comparison to Finland, East Germany, or for that matter, most of the developed world, Kenya, Ethiopia, Uganda and Tanzania have practically no money to spend on sport. There isn't a single track in the whole region with an artificial surface.

So if it's not the usual incentives of material gain or national recognition

---

*While East Africa as a geographic term commonly refers to Kenya, Uganda and Tanzania, for purposes of this essay, East Africa is defined as four countries: Kenya, Uganda, Tanzania and Ethiopia.

that have generated all the East African running success, what is it? The conventional wisdom is summed up in a word: altitude.

All the East African runners of world class were, indeed, born and raised at mile-high altitudes, and the common assumption is that this background has endowed them with superior powers of endurance, acquired either during the runners' own lifetimes or through the inheritance of traits adapted over centuries to high-altitude living. In their *Guinness Book of Olympic Records,* Norris and Ross McWhirter account for Kipchoge Keino's 3:34.9 1500 meters victory in Mexico City in a single sentence: "Còming from a Kenyan people who have lived for generations at high altitudes, he had a genetic advantage over lowlanders." With all due respect to the McWhirters, it's not quite that simple.

East Africans are far from unique in having lived for generations at high altitudes. What about the peoples of Rwanda, Lesotho, Ecuador, Tibet and Nepal, not to mention many South Africans, Peruvians, Chileans, Mexicans and Colombians? None of these peoples seem to have developed the putative "genetic advantage" in running. In fact, the only high-altitude dwellers who collectively have made any mark in the track world come from peoples living in a region that extends from the headwaters of the Blue Nile in the Ethiopian highlands south along the western rim of the Great Rift Valley through western Kenya and eastern Uganda into northern Tanzania. They all live in savanna and hill country at altitudes ranging from 5000 to 8000 feet above sea level.

But all over East Africa there are dozens of peoples living at these altitudes. The world-class runners come from only a few. The connection between those few peoples may have to do with more than just altitude and geography.

PRE-COLONIAL HISTORY OF EAST AFRICA

The pre-colonial history of East Africa has been pieced together chiefly from contemporary linguistic and cultural data, together with tribal folklore and scattered archaeological finds. It is generally agreed that the present population of the region grew out of three waves of immigration: a linguistic group known as Cushites, classed racially as Caucasoid, spread south out of the Ethiopian highlands along the Rift Valley as far as what is now northern Tanzania; they were followed by another linguistic group called Nilotes, a tall, slender Negroid subrace, who moved south-east out of what is now the Sudan into northern and eastern Uganda, western Kenya and northern Tanzania, mixing with the Cushites already in the Rift Valley area; the third linguistic group, the Bantu, also classed racially as Negroid, came from the west and south and spread throughout most of what is now Tanzania, Uganda and Kenya.

Today, the vast majority of the peoples in East Africa south of Ethiopia are Bantu speakers, but, with one major exception, the peoples from among whom the world-class runners have emerged are generally labelled Cushitic or Nilotic, or a "mixture" of the two. In Ethiopia, where the dominant group is the Amhara, classed linguistically as Semitic, most of the runners come from a numerous, widely dispersed Cushitic speaking group called the Galla. Abebe Bikila, Mamo Wolde, Shibiru Regassa and Hailu Ebba are Galla, while Miruts Yifter comes from another Cushitic group called the Beja.

Map of East Africa showing the Great Rift Valley and the location of the tribes which have produced outstanding runners.

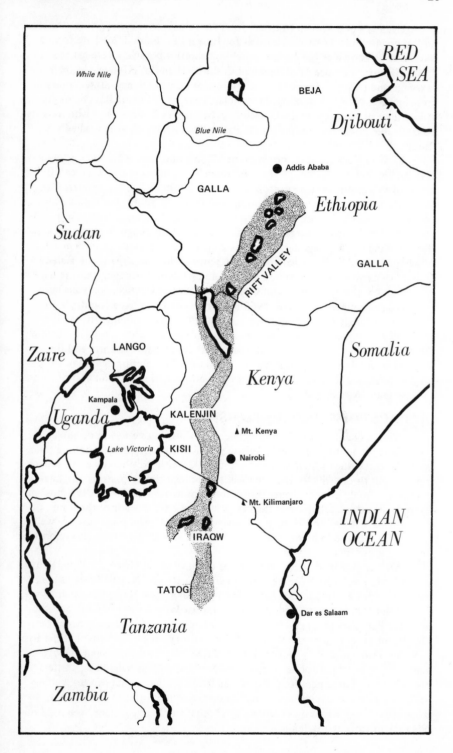

Uganda's best known runners—John Akii-Bua, Silver Ayoo, Amos Omolo and Aggri Awori (a 14-second hurdler for Harvard in the mid-'60s) are from a Nilotic tribe known as the Lango, which some anthropologists have classed as "Nilo-Hamitic" because of evidence of Cushitic (Hamitic) influence in their language and culture. Lucas Oloo, a 4:03 miler now at Oregon State, comes from another Nilotic group, the Japadhola. Tanzania's Filbert Bayi belongs to a tribe called the Iraqw who are classed linguistically as Cushitic, but who have had considerable inter-marriage with a Nilotic or "Nilo-Hamite" group called the Tatog.

Most of Kenya's best known runners also come from a Nilotic or "Nilo-Hamitic" group, the Kalenjin. The Tanzanian Tatog are thought to be an off-shoot of this group, which anthropologist G.P. Murdock has characterized as "strongly Cushitized" Nilotes, revealing "evidences of admixture with a Caucasoid racial element." Kipchoge Keino, Ben Jipcho, Mike Boit, Julius Sang, Wilson Kiprugut, John Kipkurgat, Amos Biwott, Benjamin Kogo, William Koskei, Fatwell Kimaiyo, Wesley Maiyo, Joshua Kimeto, Naftali Bon, Cosmas Sielei, Mike Murei, Kipkemboi Yego and both Ngenos (John and Kip) are all Kalenjin. In fact, so narrowly concentrated is the running talent in Kenya, that the winners of all 45 of the Olympic and Commonwealth track medals Kenyans have collected since independence in 1963 belong to just two of the country's 30-odd tribal groups: the Kalenjin and the Kisii. The two "running tribes" live next to one another in an area about the size of Los Angeles County in the highlands of western Kenya between the eastern shore of Lake Victoria and the western escarpment of the Rift Valley. Together they number less than two million people—about 15% of Kenya's population—and more than half of them are less than 16 years old.

A "RACE" OF SUPER-RUNNERS?

This concentration of running talent, not just in one region or one country, but in a few minority cultural-linguistic groups who marry chiefly among themselves, suggests the existence of some kind of Cushitic-Nilotic "race" of super-runners. Both the Nilotes and the Cushites are historically pastoral and have wandered widely after their herds over much of eastern Africa, for the most part at high altitudes. Perhaps over the centuries they have developed the kind of "genetic advantage" the McWhirters suggest—physiological traits that are well adapted to survival in a nomadic society at high altitudes, and are also important to running ability.

On the face of it, this theory seems to make sense. Even the Kisii, Kenya's second "running tribe," can be made to fit the pattern. Naftali Temu, Robert Ouko, Charles Asati, Richard Juma, Evans Mogaka, Paul Mose, Hezekiah Nyamau, John Mwebi, Arere Anentia and Nyandika Maiyoro are all Kisii, and the Kisii are Bantu speakers and historically agricultural. This would seem to be a significant exception to the Cushitic-Nilotic theory, but it happens that the Kisii have been surrounded by Nilotes for centuries, have adopted a semi-pastoral economy, and have raided for cattle back and forth with their neighbors, particularly the Kalenjin. For generations, women and children have been captured along with cattle on these raids, and there has been frequent inter-marriage, so it can be argued, if not altogether convincingly*, that the Kisii get their "genetic" running talent from the Kalenjin.

The trouble with any such theory about groups of hereditary super-runners is that there is no physiological evidence to support it. At the time of the Mexico City Olympics, *Sports Illustrated* reported that a team of German physiologists was making exhaustive studies of Kenyan and Ethiopian distance runners. But apparently all they were able to establish was that the East African athletes had the same slender physiques as most successful distance runners, and the same high aerobic capacity (the ability of the heart and lungs to make efficient use of available oxygen) as any well-conditioned athlete, or for that matter anyone who has lived a strenuous life at high altitudes for a number of years.

Nevertheless, speculation about the East Africans' hereditary running ability continues. Most often, such speculation focuses on the Nandi, a constituent tribe of the Kalenjin group in Kenya, among whom running talent seems to be most concentrated. Though the Nandi people number only about 250,000, Nandi runners have won nearly as many Olympic and Commonwealth medals in the past 10 years as all the runners from the rest of non-Kenyan Africa put together. Nandi runners include Keino, Boit, Kipkurgat, Biwott, Kogo, Koskei, Bon, Sielei, Kimaiyo, Maiyo, Kimeto, Murei, Yego, Julius Sang and Mark Sang (no relation)— all from a population of fewer than 100,000 adult males!

THE AMATEUR PHYSIOLOGICAL THEORIZING

Efforts to account for these extraordinary figures are a common pastime among followers of East African track; amateur physiological theorizing is rife. Kenya's outspoken one-time national track coach, an Englishman named John Velzian, was quick to offer his views to one reporter, "Among certain tribes," said Velzian, "there is a better ratio of leg length to overall body height. I can stand next to a Nandi athlete of the same height as myself and his navel will be two inches higher than mine." (Velzian stands 5'7" tall, and has the broad shoulders and long torso of the pole vaulter he once was.) Other amateur hypotheses suggest that the ratio of the length of the femur to the length of the lower leg bones is unusually high among the Nandi, or that the heel bone, to which the achilles tendon is attached, is unusually long, thus giving runners extra leverage. But there are no systematically gathered data that indicate that leg bones are of unusual lengths among the Nandi or any other "running" tribe. What's more, most physiological research to date on the length of the leg bones among runners indicates that there is no statistically significant correlation between leg length and running success.

In order to prove that the evident running talent of many Nandis is due to the special genetic endowment of the Nandi people, research would have to isolate at least one physiological trait that was present in the "modal" (average in terms of physiological measurements) Nandi—not just the successful runners—and

*Another Bantu group, the Luhya, are also surrounded by Nilotes, against whom they have raided back and forth for cattle, but though they excel at soccer, no Luhya has yet become a world class runner. Yet another Kenya Bantu group, the Kamba, far on the other side of the Rift Valley, are represented by several international runners like Philip Ndoo, Francis Musyoki, Patrick Kiingi, and James Munyala. Even the Kikuyu, the Bantu group who are politically dominant in Kenya, but who are held to take little interest in sports, have turned out a few distinguished athletes, among them, Wilson Waigwa, currently a star miler at the University of Texas at El Paso.

absent in modal members of tribes that haven't produced runners. Then research would have to establish that the trait was genetically determined and that it was instrumental in running ability. So far, no such trait has been isolated, and it is unlikely that any ever will be.

Even for a trait such as blood type, which is easily isolated and unquestionably a function of specific genes, it has been difficult to establish variations that are consistent with tribal differences. This is because tribes are not based on hereditary or blood ties; a tribe is simply a group of people who share a common culture, and particularly a common language. East African historian J. E. G. Sutton puts it quite simply: "A tribe is a tribe because it feels it is one . . . There is no such thing as a pure tribe derived from a single founding ancestor." Tribes, Sutton adds, are fluid groupings: "Some members are lost, others are absorbed, through the continual processes of migration and interaction with neighbors . . . A tribe emerges not by maintaining the pure blood of its ancestors, not by sedulously avoiding contact with its neighbors, but by successfully assimilating its diverse elements. To survive, a tribe must continually adjust itself to surrounding circumstances."

CULTURAL, ENVIRONMENTAL DATA

Rather than speculate further about possible "genetic advantages" the East African runners may or may not have been blessed with, it's probably more fruitful to examine available cultural and environmental data, which can, at least, be substantiated, to try to account for their running success.

The East African runners were, after all, raised at high altitudes, and most of them spent much of their youths chasing up and down hills after cattle and goats, or, more recently, running long distances to school. Kieno, Jipcho, Temu, Bayi and others recall racing miles to school to avoid being late and getting caned by their strict schoolmasters.

The diet of the "running" peoples is spare and quite starchy, but it does contain a rather high proportion of protein relative to the diets of other African peoples. Both the Cushites and Nilotes are historically pastoral, and milk is still one of the staple foods among many present day Cushitic and Nilotic peoples. The Kalenjin have traditionally regarded milk as sacred, and drink large amounts whenever it is available, the greatest quantities going to the young men. A delicacy among the Kalenjin is milk that has been aged and curdled in a calabash cured with cow urine and the ashes of a bush known as the *senetwet*. The resulting lumpy liquid, *mursik*, has the look of runny blueberry yogurt, but its taste is rather more sour.

(A photograph well known in Kenya shows Kipchoge Keino just off the plane from the Mexico City Olympics drinking *mursik* from a calabash handed him by a Kalenjin well-wisher. Keino's own surname relates to milk. Properly "arap Keino," it means he is the son of a man born when goats were being milked.

The magnificently built Nandi runner John Kipkurgat, 800-meter sensation at the '74 Commonwealth Games where he led almost all the way to win in 1:43.9, with his tribesman Mike Boit second in 1:44.4. Boit feels that Kipkurgat, who was 29 when he won his Commonwealth Games' gold medal, has the potential to run 1:40 for the 800 meters! (Mark Shearman)

His first name, Kipchoge, means that he himself was born near his family's grain store, and his son's surname, bestowed after initiation, will be arap Choge, son of a man born near the grain store. "Kip Keino," the name the runner is widely known by in the Western press is, in fact, his father's first name (one word: Kip-keino). The runner himself is properly addressed only as arap Keino by other Kalenjin, except his parents and friends of their generation, who may call him Kipchoge. "Kipchoge" is frequently used in the Kenya press because, by coincidence, the word "keino" is an offensive vulgarism in the language of the Kikuyu, President Jomo Kenyatta's tribe. The names of other Kalenjin runners are also confused in the press, though matters of delicacy are not usually the reason. Wilson Kiprugut, twice an Olympic 800-meter medalist, is properly Wilson Kiprugut arap Chumo. His sons will be arap Rugut after they are initiated.)

On special occasions, the Kalenjin and a few other running tribes mix milk with blood drawn by an expert bowman from the jugular of a young heifer. Not surprisingly, when Kipchoge Keino inadvertently revealed on his first trip to the US that his people occasionally drank blood, sensation-hungry journalists immediately began attributing his extraordinary performances to this custom, characterizing the young Kenyan as some kind of a cross between Superman and Dracula.

STOICAL ENDURANCE THROUGH TRADITIONAL CULTURE?

In addition to the altitude, the activity of the herd boys and the relatively protein rich diet, all of which are common to dozens of peoples, not just those that the runners come from, there are several features of the traditional cultures of the running tribes which may have contributed to the development of their runners. Anthropologist A.H. Barclay has examined such practices among the Nandi. Barclay suggests that Nandi men are conditioned from an early age to solitary, stoical endurance of pain—just the sort of discipline required of middle and long distance runners. As adolescents, all Nandi must undergo slow and painful ritual circumcision under the eyes of a watchful crowd of elders in order to be initiated into adulthood. If a boy should so much as blink in pain during the operation, he will be labelled *kipite*, to his eternal shame, and be denied full rights as a Nandi adult. In some areas in earlier times, the scrutiny of the initiates was said to have been so close that the boys' faces were caked with mud before the operation and if the smallest crack appeared on the dried mud during the cutting, the offender was automatically *kipite*.

Ritual circumcision as an initiation rite is common to all the East African running peoples except the Lango, through in several cases the initiate's ordeal is somewhat less taxing. The Lango remove the two central lower incisors as an initiation rite. This practice is shared by most Nilotic peoples, as well as the Iraqw, but among some, like the Kalenjin, it no longer has ritual significance and is said to be a precaution against starvation in the event of lockjaw.

Another practice common to all the East African running peoples is the division of the society into age sets, social role groupings loosely based on age. One of the age sets invariably functions as the tribe's active warriors, and this group jealously guards its status from the encroachment of its juniors. Among the Nandi, for example, a young man reaches the status of *murenet,* or warrior, some years after his initiation. In pre-colonial times this meant that he was allowed to join raiding parties which would venture into the territory of neighboring tribes to "re-possess" cattle the Nandi felt were theirs by divine right. The raids were conducted largely at night and sometimes ranged over distances as great as 100 miles! Most raiding parties were group ventures but each *murenet* was expected to at least do his share. According to Samuel K. arap Ngeny, a Nandi historian, "No warrior was worthy of his name unless he had distinguished himself in one of these raids."

The more cattle a *murenet* managed to bring back with him, the more he increased not only his own prestige, and the prestige of the *murenik* (pl.), but also his own wealth. If he had cattle of his own, he might be able to buy himself a wife or two.* These were no doubt powerful incentives for *murenik* to become successful cattle raiders, and Barclay's point is that the same energies elicited by these incentives were later re-channeled onto the track after the Colonial Government put an effective stop to cattle raiding.

The weakness of this argument is that circumcision, cattle raiding and competition among age sets, which Barclay suggests encouraged the Nandi to develop habits of stoical endurance and self-reliance useful to them as runners, are not unique to the Nandi, or even to the East African running tribes. Barclay stresses the unusual severity of the Nandi circumcision, the extraordinary prestige given the raiding *murenik* in Nandi society, and the exceptional strenuousness of their long-distance raids. But the fact remains that ritual circumcision is used as an initiation into adulthood by most of the tribes in Kenya, as well as by scores of cultures throughout Africa and the world, and cattle raiding was so common among several tribes in Kenya when the British arrived that they made stopping it one of their first governmental priorities. A number of the peoples in East Africa and elsewhere who practice circumcision and once raided for livestock also are pastoralists, some living at high altitudes, but only a few have produced world class runners.

It may, however, be significant that in Kenya, at least, one of the ways the Colonial Administration tried to stop cattle raiding was to introduce athletics as a surrogate. Oxbridge-trained District Officers marked out dozens of uneven grass tracks on pasture land all over the Colony. Eventually, a pyramid system of regional athletics meetings was set up throughout Kenya, and later Uganda and Tanzania as well. Local meets were held every year on successive Saturdays in July, each meet taking in progressively larger administrative regions and culminating in the three National Championships, and by the 1950s, the East African Championships.

In local meetings, prizes such as blankets, lamps and cooking pots were given to winners, as it was assumed that Africans could not be induced to make a sincere effort merely for the glory of it. But in some areas, officials tried to get young warriors to regard athletic competition as a means of winning the prestige

---

* This aspect of the practice of cattle raiding offers some theoretical support to those who believe that Nandi running abilities are the result of their "genetic advantage." If the runner with the greatest stamina became the most successful cattle raider and was thereby able to buy himself the most wives, it follows that the best runners had the most children, and the worst runners either captured too few cattle to be able to afford wives or were themselves captured or killed by enemy tribes during raids. Thus it can be argued that cattle raiding acted as a powerful genetic selection mechanism, favoring strong runners.

they would otherwise have earned in cattle raids. Arthur Walford, a teacher for many years under the colonial administration in Kenya, recalled one such campaign in the late 1930s among the Kipsigis, another constituent tribe of the Kalenjin group (John Ngeno is a Kipsigis). "At that time an attempt was being made to stop the Kipsigis from persistent cattle raiding . . . with the slogan (translated from the Kipsigis) 'Show your valor in sports and games, not in war.' Unfortunately, the Second World War started soon after this laudable precept had begun to take hold and it had to be put into reverse in order to recruit for the K.A.R. (King's African Rifles)."

One of the reasons why the precept had begun to take hold is that before the crash war-time enlistment drive, athletic achievement had been one of the chief routes into the Army. Young warriors may not have seen track meets as an adequate substitute for the prohibited cattle raids, but many could see beyond the blankets and cooking pots to the security of a uniformed job in the Army or Police, with a regular cash income—increasingly a necessity in the fast-changing society of colonial East Africa.

IMPORTANT ROLE OF THE ARMED FORCES

It is difficult to over-estimate the importance of East Africa's various armed forces in developing the area's running talent, and it is worth noting that members of the "running tribes" are represented in the uniformed services of three of the countries in numbers out of all proportion to their share of each country's total population. In Ethiopia, Abebe Bikila and Mamo Wolde were both members of what was once Emperor Haile Selassie's Palace Body Guard, Miruts Yifter is in the Air Force and other runners have come from Ethiopia's Army, where the Galla make up a disproportionately large segment of the corps of enlisted men. There is no evidence of tribal imbalance in the Tanzanian People's Defense Force, in which Filbert Bayi serves as an Air Force Technician, but in Uganda, where John Akii-Bua is an officer in the Police, and other runners like Silver Ayoo are in the uniformed Prisons Service, the Lango were over-represented in the Army as a result of deliberate moves by former President Milton Obote, a Lango, to surround himself with his fellow tribesmen. The Lango were almost completely driven out of the Army after General Amin's takeover in 1971.

In Kenya, nearly every one of the country's best known athletes has spent at least some time in one of the uniformed services: the Army, Police, Prison Service, and G.S.U. (General Service Unit—a kind of Presidential riot squad). Since early colonial times, the Kalenjin have been vastly over-represented in both the Army and the Police. This may have been because both organizations actively recruited athletes from about the time of the First World War, and in the process of colony-wide enlistment, they may have come upon an obvious font of talent in the Kalenjin area, and after that concentrated their activities there. But at least in part, the Kalenjin seem to have been recruited because the British had a peculiar admiration for them.

THE NANDI—LEAN, SPARTAN AND PROUD

The Nandi in particular were much esteemed by the British civil servants, who came to Kenya as colonial officers fresh from the rigors of the army or ascetic public schools, and were well disposed to admire a lean, Spartan bunch like these highland pastoralists. In the eyes of the middle-class Englishman, the stoical, spear-carrying *murenet* seems to have embodied the dignity and power of Rousseau's noble savage, together with the restraint and decorum of a black-skinned Edwardian gentleman. E. T. Harris, a colonial community development officer among the Nandi for seven years, put it this way: "One must stress the independence of the Nandi people. They were an aristocratic group with a very decided culture of their own. How many small ethnic entities regard themselves as really "it" in the world they know of? (The British have not failed themselves by not thinking of themselves in this way.)"

When the British first arrived in Kenya at the end of the 19th century, the Nandi fought fiercely to resist foreign encroachment on what had been their open grazing land. The *murenik* would tear up the rails of the railroad the British were building and melt them down for weapons to use against the invaders. But the Nandi resistance only served to endear them further to their colonial masters once they'd finally been conquered. Harris remarked: "The British had to quell these unruly people. It appears that the arrogance common to both parties quickly led to mutual respect, for by the 1914-18 war, these very 'backward' people (the Kalenjin) became an important element in the British army, serving with bravery and becoming the largest component in the Kenyan African Rifles and the Kenya Police."

Once in East Africa's various armed forces, potential runners, particularly the athletic recruits, got the encouragement, discipline and time—if not always the coaching—they needed to develop whatever talents they had. Since independence, incentives and opportunities for successful athletes have widened, particularly in Kenya. Strong rivalries have developed between the armed services, so that athletes are even more actively recruited by the various branches. Moreover, in a country whose first development priority is education, many schools offer inducements to athletes. Primary schools often allow outstanding athletes to repeat a year in order to get just one more chance to pass the highly competitive Certificate exam and qualify for secondary school. Sports-oriented secondary schools compete to enroll promising primary school athletes, often regardless of whether or not they have passed their exams. Teacher training colleges recruit athletes from the secondary schools, and now, for a few, there are even athletic scholarships to American universities. Furthermore, as Kenya's stature as an international track power has grown, more and more Kenyans are competing abroad, and the prospect of foreign travel and its attendant material rewards ("expense" money, free equipment) is alive in the imagination of many a promising young runner.

These proliferating rewards and opportunities are open to everyone in Kenya, and they have generated somewhat more wide-spread interest in track, but so far, much like the Olympic medals, these more functional prizes have gone disproportionately to the same two minority peoples: the Kalenjin and the Kisii. Perhaps it was the example of the first Army and Police athletic recruits that started it, but since early colonial times these two groups have dominated not just international competition, but regional, school and armed services meets as well. By the 1950s, the effects of the repeated successes were snowballing, and there is no question that self-perpetuating traditions of athletic achievement were firmly established in the Kalenjin and Kisii areas at the time of independence. Similar traditions have developed in Uganda among the Lango and one or two other Nilotic groups.

So it can be argued that the continued athletic dominance of a few of the running tribes is due at least in part to self-fulfilling expectations that they have about their own ability. People from other tribes all over Kenya and Uganda have similar expectations about the Kalenjin, the Kisii and the Lango, so that if, for example, a young Nandi boy goes to school outside his district, he will be expected to be a runner—and an extraordinary number of such "expatriate" schoolboys from the running tribes do become fine athletes, a much bigger proportion, in fact, than among their tribesmen back in their own home districts.

A similar argument of self-fulfilling expectations is advanced by American sociologists like Harry Edwards to explain the dominance of US blacks in sprints, horizontal jumps and hurdling events in American track and field, where the material incentives for achievement (apart from college scholarships) are somewhat less obvious than they are in sports that are played professionally.

But in East Africa, the mere fact that boys from certain tribes say to themselves, "My people are good runners, so I should be a good runner," doesn't seem adequate to account for 19 medals in running events at the last two Olympics, won for the most part without benefit of professional full-time coaching, proper diet or equipment, or what Western runners would consider anything like adequate training, by runners from a few peoples in four developing countries.

Why is it just those few peoples? What started the snowball of their expectations rolling? Is the answer altitude? The rigors of their up-bringing? Selective encouragement by the colonial power? Or do these people have a "genetic advantage"?

We probably won't ever know. Among the first aims of each of the governments in the developing countries of East Africa is the promotion of national unity, and research that stresses differences among a country's people is not likely to be welcomed. Outsiders will have to be content to admire the magnificent East African runners, and not to reason why.

Kisii runners Paul Mose (416) and Richard Juma (405) closely follow world record holder Dave Bedford in the '74 Commonwealth Games 10,000. The third Kenyan is Patrick Kiingi, a Kamba. (Mark Shearman)

Chapter Four

Science on the Altitude Factor
by Dr. Jack Daniels

[**Editor:** The idea that altitude training offers great advantages in the endurance running events and that high-altitude natives have a natural physiological advantage over their sea-level opponents originated with the late Abebe Bikila's surprising marathon victory in the 1960 Olympics. The breakthrough of the Kenyan runners in the mid-'60s was seen as further proof of this theory. No less an authority than John Velzian, Kenya's national coach in the mid-'60s, cited altitude as possibly the main reason for the success of Kenya's athletes.

Speaking specifically about the Kalenjin athletes, Velzian wrote in the British publication *World Sports* in 1967: "There are a number of reasons for (their) success... They were born and have lived all their lives at an altitude well above 5000 feet. This operates to their advantage in several ways. Since their whole physiology of respiration has become adapted to living in an atmosphere with a decreased supply of oxygen, it is of considerable benefit to them when competing at lower levels—a reversal of the factors which handicap the low-altitude athlete when competing higher up..." (Note that this analysis was made a full year before the high-altitude runners of Kenya and Ethiopia ran wild in the distance events at the Mexico City Olympics.)

Today it's safe to say that most runners, coaches and track fans in the US and other established track and field nations of the world believe in the theory so well summed up by Velzian. But what does science have to say on the subject? Is there any *scientific* evidence to support the widely-held notions that a life at altitude is the "key" to the success of the African distance runners, and that the high-altitude native (or the sea-level native trained at altitude, for that matter) has a physiological advantage generally over the runner trained at sea level?

If anyone is qualified to speak from a scientific point of view on altitude training and distance running, it's Dr. Jack Daniels, physiologist and track coach at the University of Texas in Austin. Dr. Daniels did extensive research on altitude training before the '68 Olympics, working with many of the finest runners in the US, including Jim Ryun, George Young and Tom von Ruden, and he probably knows more about altitude training than any other physiologist in the US. Here, with the African runners in mind, Dr. Daniels discusses what research tells us (and doesn't tell us) about altitude training and distance running.]

When the International Olympic Committee chose Mexico City as the site of the 1968 Summer Olympics, few athletes, officials or coaches felt much immediate panic even though some knowledgeable scientists expressed concern over the effects of Mexico's 7400-foot altitude. After all, Mexico had hosted the 1955 Pan-American Games and even though there were some drastically slower times in endurance races there were also some excellent performances, by any standards, in events not requiring prolonged performance at high energy expenditure. The fact that only North, South and Central Americans were involved in the Pan-American Games probably contributed considerably to a lack of concern, since distance runners from these areas were not particularly noted for their prowess in the mid-'50s and consequently slow times were taken lightly. Only the participants were in a position to know the consequences of racing at altitude without prior training in the thinner air, and their reactions were most likely considered all part of being "psyched out" by the altitude.

Then came the 1968 Olympics and the distance events were dominated by runners who had spent most of their lives at altitude. Early warnings that athletes would die at Mexico City's altitude were replaced by cries that altitude natives were at a great and unfair advantage at the Olympics, at least in all the distance running events. The results seemed to bear this out. African runners seemed to be controlling the longer races, running and winning almost as they pleased.

The big question is, were the Africans winning only because of the altitude or would they have won regardless of the altitude? I don't think the answer will ever be known, at least as it may have applied to Mexico City in 1968. African distance runners had already begun to show tremendous talent for long races, the altitude at Mexico City provided the extra psychological boost necessary to convince them that they really were equal to or better than the rest of the world.

The biggest psychological advantage at altitude that African runners would seem to have had over sea-level residents is their increased self-confidence compared to that of their opponents. For example, at sea level Jim Ryun had a great deal of confidence in his ability to beat Kip Keino and Keino probably had "N" amount of confidence in his ability to beat Ryun. At altitude, however, even if Ryun had just as much confidence in his chances of victory, Keino undoubtedly had "N + X" confidence in his own chances which could easily spell the difference in the outcome of a race between two nearly-equal athletes under normal conditions. Whether more altitude races for Ryun and the other sea-level competitors under various race and pace patterns in the two or three years prior to 1968 would have changed the result of the 1500 can only be guessed. Certainly the race as it was run (i.e. an extremely fast early pace) was a first for the sea-level competitors, and even if it was also a first for the altitude runners, then their increased self-confidence could have carried them through.

Actually, the physiological adjustments that take place during acclimatization to altitude are not totally mysterious in nature, nor have they been adequately investigated. However, enough basic information was available prior to the 1968 Olympics Games so that sea-level athletes should have been able to participate in Mexico with a certain degree of confidence. Unfortunately, most sea-level runners were not completely prepared for their races at altitude, but more from a standpoint of inadequate *competitive* acclimatization than from inadequate *physiological* adjustment. The African runners, on the other hand, had both going for them?

I don't think there was an American middle or long distance runner who was as ready as he should have, or could have, been for his race in Mexico. For a non-acclimatized miler to race a mile at altitude would be similar, from a competitive standpoint, to having him race a sea-level two-mile for the first time. It's a different race and requires some adjustment. A miler running a two-mile for the first time may do a good job, but not as good as after he's raced the distance several times. The same thing applies at altitude: the mile is not the same race it is at sea level and no matter how well conditioned the runner is, he won't have complete confidence in himself in that new race until he's raced it under various conditions and situations, i.e. with a fast start, a burst in the middle, or a slow pace and fast finish. How early can he afford to go for the finish? What if some rabbit sets out faster than anticipated? Are the prelims more tiring or less tiring at altitude? Maybe the conditions are so different that a sea-level miler would be a better altitude 5000-meter man, or vice versa. *Training* at altitude doesn't answer these questions. *Racing* at altitude would help considerably. *Race acclimatization* for sea-level athletes was not what it should have been for Mexico '68.

Following our Mexico City experiences, defeats and increased research at altitude, what have we learned that can be applied to future training? First of all, we have learned that it is necessary for sea-level residents to engage in serious preparations farther in advance than a few months, should a similar circumstance arise. Secondly, I would hope that some champion athletes native to altitude could be compared with sea-level natives who also enjoy success in endurance events. Do the altitude natives have definite physiological advantages over their sea-level counterparts? It is probably impossible to provide a simple or completely accurate answer to this question. To start with, the question should be phrased in more specific terms, as a two-part question: (1) Do altitude natives have an advantage over sea-level natives in an altitude race? (2) Do altitude natives have an advantage over sea-level natives in a sea-level race?

LOOKING FOR THE ANSWERS

Where does one look for the answers to these questions? At the results of Mexico '68? If so, it seems clear that the answer to question number one is yes. Yet how many sea-level Olympians in Mexico had been well prepared, if prepared

Kipchoge Keino is one stride away from completing his fantastic 3:34.9 1500 meters (after a first 800 meters of 1:55.3) at the Mexico City Olympics. His time, which was only 1.8 seconds off the world record, was faster than people believed humanly possible at Mexico City's 7400-foot altitude. Jim Ryun finished second, about 20 yards behind Keino, in 3:37.8. (Ed Lacey)

at all, for an altitude race? What other altitude competitions do we have for making comparisons? Probably none where the sea-level runners made any serious altitude preparations. So from a competitive point of view we have insufficicient evidence.

What about research? Based on the findings of a variety of studies at various altitudes, it appears that growing up at altitude can increase the total lung surface area in animals; it leads to a greater diffusion capacity across the lung walls into the blood; it lowers the critical pressure of oxygen at which the individual passes out or becomes incapacitated; it lowers the body's sensitivity to hypoxia (or lowered oxygen pressure) found at altitude so that ventilation is less for altitude natives. The big question is: do any of these apparent differences aid performance? In other words, are these differences important determinants of success in a race?

We think of larger lungs, greater lung-blood gas-exchange area, greater diffusion capacity as desirable factors for better performance. If more oxygen can be presented to the blood in the lungs in a shorter time it would seem to be advantageous. However, this is only true if one could take advantage of this improvement. At sea level there is a good chance that these would *not* be advantageous because the blood must carry the oxygen to the working muscles via the cardiovascular, oxygen transport system. If the blood is fully saturated with oxygen with a given set of lungs (as it is with healthy sea-level athletes) it can't become more than fully saturated just by presenting it with more oxygen. However, when the conditions are such that getting adequate oxygen from the atmosphere into the blood becomes a limiting factor (as it may be during hard work at altitude), then we may have a difference between the sea-level and altitide residents. So an athlete acclimatized to altitude would have a real advantage over a non-acclimatized athlete in an altitude race.

Another adjustment to residence at altitude is an increase in hemoglobin in the blood—the substance responsible for carrying oxygen in the blood. An increase in hemoglobin should be advantageous for an endurance race since the oxygen carrying capacity of the blood is consequently improved. Again, however, we can carry this a step further and question whether transporting more oxygen to the working tissues is beneficial if the muscle cells can only use a limited amount of the oxygen presented to them. Chances are cellular utilization of oxygen will change with exposure to the hypoxia of altitude, so again acclimatized athletes are at an advantage in an altitude race. What seems quite clear and widely accepted is that altitude-acclimatized runners are at a distinct advantage in a race being run at altitude. What about the African altitude native who comes to sea level to race? Does he have an advantage there also?

Again, we can look at results of important races and research. Munich Olympic results would suggest that the Africans didn't do nearly as well in terms of medals won as in Mexico City four years earlier. But other results at sea level could be interpreted either way, with excellent middle- and long-distance results having been turned in by African and non-African runners. To further cloud the issue, more and more sea-level athletes include altitude training in their programs so it becomes more difficult to make meaningful comparisons.

The results of research involving the effects of training at altitude on sea-level performance show that there are different individual reactions to spending time at altitude. Athletes who have demonstrated outstanding ability at sea level, but who are not in top form show definite and rapid improvement in sea level performance following altitude training. Some "peak-conditioned" runners have also shown improvements after a time at altitude, but the mechanism responsible for the change is not clear. An increase in aerobic capacity may or may not be apparent. Greater anaerobic involvement would seem more likely as a result of learning to push harder, subjectively, while at altitude. This subjective "toughness" may then carry over for a time back at sea level. Again, the duration of these changes may be short-lived, especially if competitive situations are not in abundance at sea level. African runners who have grown up competing under the stress of altitude may very well be able to accept more discomfort in a sea-level race than would the average sea-level native, with the result that a faster early pace or a demanding burst during a long race would be accepted with less anxiety than it might be by their competitors.

Regarding the question of a lasting effect of altitude training after moving to (or back to) sea level, consideration must be given to the period of time spent at altitude. More important may be the period of one's life which was spent at altitude. Being at altitude during the period of time when body growth is greatest may bring about certain anatomical changes which can't take place later in life, regardless of how hard the training. Maybe living and training at altitude during growth is the only combination which results in advantages, or disadvantages, in performance later in life. Regardless of why an anatomical change may result from a childhood at altitude, these attributes will most likely remain changed indefinitely.

On the other hand, some differences noted between sea-level and altitude athletes are presumably strictly the result of the lower barometric pressure at altitude and moving from one environment to the other will result in a certain adjustment or "acclimatization" to the new environment. Chances are that most of these transient changes take place relatively rapidly (usually within a period of weeks).

Athletes often "feel" better after training at altitude. For the African runner at sea level, this again may be a factor which contributes to success, just as does the willingness to push harder in a race. There is no question that a race at sea level is a relative joy following training at altitude. This is especially true if the initial pace at sea level is not much different from the accepted altitude pace. It's only logical that halfway through a sea-level race, the altitude athlete will be feeling as though the pace should be increased a bit. An African altitude runner is almost certain to beat all his previous performances in his initial sea-level competitions. This fact alone builds confidence in producing continued improvements.

BEST TYPE OF TRAINING AT ALTITUDE

One question to which little attention has been paid is that regarding the type of training best suited for the altitude native. Whether African runners should train similarly at altitude and sea level hasn't been investigated either. One can perhaps best get the answers to these questions by looking at what we know about the type of training a sea-level athlete should do if he goes up to altitude.

In the latter case, the type of training will have to be carefully chosen so as not to allow a diminution of condition. Detraining of certain systems could take

place over a long period at altitude if normal training habits are abandoned. This would be most apparent in mechanical efficiency and muscular power. For example, a four-minute miler who at sea level normally runs 15 interval quarters at 60 seconds each with 60-second rests in between will undoubtedly have to adjust the speed of the intervals if he still wants to run 15 quarters with the same 60-second recovery at altitude. If normal recovery periods are maintained between 15 quarters, chances are the speed will be closer to 65 than 60. Over longer-distance intervals the usual speed will be even more difficult to maintain. Running the intervals at slower speeds over a long period of training could easily result in a 60-second pace being too fast or uncomfortable back at sea-level, even when the oxygen-transport system is at full capacity. The reason for the stress would be lack of practice at the desired competitive intensity or speed.

If anything should be changed at altitude it most likely should be the recovery interval between work bouts. If it needs to be longer, in order to insure normal training intensity, then that's the most logical adjustment. After all, with a lowered aerobic capacity (as exists at altitude) the energy demands of a standard work load must be provided for more anerobically than at sea level. The greater anerobic involvement means a little more recovery is necessary to restore an equal state of physiological readiness as would normally be desired before starting the next work session. This would suggest that runners training at altitude would benefit more from high quality interval work than from bulk mileage or longer, sustained hard runs. This mainly applies to relatively accomplished competitors who have already reached a high level of competency, whether they be altitude Africans or sea-level athletes training at altitude.

In a sense, altitude training is simply another form of training. It does place additional stresses on various systems of the body, but possibly no greater stress than does very intense training at sea level. Very possibly this factor accounts for the individual differences in reaction to altitude training. The athlete with great genetic potential will best realize that potential through hard training. Being at altitude tends to bypass some of the needed drive to do hard work by imposing greater stresses on systems which respond favorably to the stresses, with the result that performance improves with seemingly less work. The athlete who lacks superior potential and always trains very hard for what he gets may find being at altitude adds nothing to the stresses already imposed on his system at sea level.

From this standpoint more of the "high-potential" athletes may be identified from altitude countries such as we seem to be seeing with various African nations. On the other hand, where are the champions that should be coming from high-altitude countries in South America, or the Rocky Mountains in the United States for that matter?

"African runners who have grown up competing under the stress of altitude may very well be able to accept more discomfort in a sea-level race than the average sea-level native." Kenya's Ben Jipcho follows the torrid pace of England's Brendan Foster in the '74 Commonwealth Games 5000 before outkicking Foster by a yard down the homestraight. Jipcho's winning time, 13:14.4, was the second fastest ever. (Mark Shearman)

For those who say that altitude natives have an advantage at sea level, I ask, which altitude natives? Only African? Only black? If that's the case, maybe we're barking up the wrong tree when we attribute success to a life at altitude. Some obvious racial differences do exist among athletes. For example, American Caucasians would seem to have an edge over the Japanese in fielding athletes in sports which require height, and the Japanese, in turn, would seem to have the advantage fielding athletes in sports which require a more compact physique—e.g. gymnastics. There seems to be as much evidence to support the physical inequities which exist among races as the physiological differences which might exist among inhabitants of different parts of the world.

One may also ask why the African altitude natives don't just completely destroy the world distance running records? Do you think they are playing games with the sea-level runners? You can bet they're trying as hard as they can to win and run fast. But if they have a big advantage, as altitude natives, why don't they quit fooling around with the "mundane" sea-level records and really cut loose?

This is not to say that altitude natives aren't at a true advantage either in an altitude or a sea-level endurance race. It is to say that there is need for more scientific evidence which effectively controls for all other variables before any facts can be established. However, from what little information is available, any *disadvantage* that an African runner might have in initial exposure to sea level is probably lack of races, which is easily adjusted for.

In summarizing research which deals with altitude and distance running, it is apparent that: (1) performances will be better at sea level than at altitude, for any individual; (2) growing up at altitude does produce some physiological differences which would seem to aid performance at altitude; (3) it is possible to apply normal sea-level training methods at altitude, but more attention should probably be given to "quality" work while at altitude; (4) altitude natives have less difficulty adjusting to sea-level competitions than do sea-level natives in adjusting to altitude; (5) sea-level natives can improve performance at altitude through a period of training at altitude.

Probably the biggest issue which research has *not* yet resolved is whether the African runner, or any altitude resident, has a distinct physiological advantage over a well-trained sea-level native in a race at sea level. Of course, neither has sufficient proof been provided to show that a sea-level native who trains at altitude can improve sea-level performance beyond that which could be brought about by sufficiently intense sea-level training.

My own feelings are that altitude training can and will be used to improve sea-level performances, by *some* sea-level natives. It won't help others and could actually work to the disadvantage of some. I think that many African athletes are in a desirable situation of having been able to grow up and initiate their training at moderate altitude where the combination of adequate training plus the stress of altitude have provided the right combination of factors which bring out the potential which lies within. Whether that inherent ability is any greater in Africans than in other athletes is not known. If there is a difference, it would be of great importance to determine whether to attribute the difference to racial factors or geographical residence. Whatever the reasons, I applaud the success of the African runners and am quick to attribute that success to (1) genetic endowment, (2) opportunity to train and compete, and (3) motivation. Without all of these, they wouldn't be where they are in athletics today.

Chapter Five

The Kenyan Success
by Philip Ndoo

Philip Ndoo is ideally qualified to write about Kenyan track. He's one of Kenya's finest distance runners and has represented the country internationally on several occasions (in the 1970 Commonwealth Games, he was seventh in the 10,000 in 28:42.6 and 15th in the marathon, 2:22:15). From 1969-1972, he worked as a sports reporter for Nairobi's Daily Nation, the largest English daily in East Africa. As the former secretary of the Nairobi Amateur Athletic Association, he's also experienced as an official in Kenyan track.

Since 1972, Philip, who's 29, has been on an athletic scholarship at Eastern New Mexico University in Portales, N.M., majoring in journalism and economics. After graduation in 1975, he plans to return to Nairobi to work for the Daily Nation.

His track accomplishments while at Eastern New Mexico have been considerable. In 1974, for instance, he was the NAIA steeplechase and six-mile champion, won the outstanding performer award at the Kansas Relays, and set personal bests in the mile, three-mile and six-mile (4:08.0, 13:26.0 and 28:07.8).

In Rome, Italy, in 1960, a slender, barefooted runner, moving effortlessly over the pavement, his expression calm and unchanging, won the most gruelling Olympic event of them all—the 26-mile, 385-yard marathon. It was the first time in history that a black African had won the coveted gold medal. Overnight, Abebe Bikila became a hero in Africa.

Bikila probably didn't consider himself a revolutionary. But his surprise victory in the Rome Olympics kindled the fire which was in less than a decade to spread over all of East Africa and many other parts of the continent as well. That revolution climaxed in the 1968 Olympics when five Africans, Mohamed Gammoudi, Kipchoge Keino, Mamo Wolde, Amos Biwott and Naftali Temu, emulated Bikila's performance, winning Olympic gold medals. But the critics, especially in the Western world, attributed the success of the African athletes to Mexico City's altitude. It wasn't until the 1970 Commonwealth Games in sea-level Edinburgh, Scotland, and the 1972 Olympics in Munich, West Germany, that these critics reluctantly agreed that the African athlete was for real.

One country where the revolution started by Bikila went full blast is Kenya. In less than a decade, this relatively small and young nation (approximately the size and population of Texas) has produced such a galaxy of outstanding runners as to leave the world wondering: Is the African runner man or superman?

And perhaps there is a mystery. While the rest of the world wonders how Kenya, with a population of about 11 million, produces so many fine runners, the Kenyans themselves are at a loss to explain why 90% of the country's middle and long distance runners come from the Kalenjin and Kisii tribes, two of the 38 official tribes in the country (this number could double depending on the base for determining a tribe).

The Kalenjin and Kisii are not related, nor are they the only tribes who live in high-altitude areas. The only connection between them is that they border each other. Although there is no concrete evidence, some have speculated that some Kalenjin blood has found its way into the Kisii tribe through intermarriage. However, none of the current top runners from either tribe remembers his ancestors having blood relations with Kisii/Kalenjin.

AN EXPLANATION FEW TAKE SERIOUSLY

Many observers have attributed the success of the Kisii and Kalenjin runners to the fact that these tribesmen were brought up in a tough and rugged environment where walking for miles daily was a common occurrence. But those who know the Kenyan people well are not likely to take such an explanation seriously. There is evidence to prove that other Kenyan tribes, the Masai in the south and the Galla, Boran and Rendille in the north walk longer distances on the average, in search of water for their cattle, than either the Kisii or Kalenjin. Yet, in the case of the northern tribes, not a single individual has shown any traces of possessing the athletic talents so evident among the Kisii and Kalenjin. The Masai, who are, in fact, part of the Kalenjin tribal group, have produced no outstanding runners, with the exception of 400-meter runner Daniel Rudisha.

The Masai, however, have produced remarkable high jumpers, among them the legendary Joseph Lerasae, who in 1962 set a Kenyan high jump record of 6'8", clearing the high jump bar like a farmer jumping over his fence (to paraphrase Roger Bannister's description of Amos Biwott's style in winning the steeplechase at the Mexico Olympics). His Kenyan high jump record wasn't bettered until 1970—and then by only one-quarter inch.

John Velzian has written of Lerasae: "(He) was placed only fourth in Cardiff (at the '58 Commonwealth Games), but was surely one of the world's great high jumpers of his day, for who else could have cleared this height (i.e., 6'8" in '62) from a takeoff as much as seven feet away from the bar! I am convinced that had he received only good basic coaching he could have been up among the world record breakers and, possibly, the first high jumper in the world over seven feet."

One of the unanswered questions about the Masai is why they don't dominate javelin throwing in Kenya. They not only learn the skills of handling a spear at an early age, but it is part of their lives—e.g., hunting, defending their cattle against wild animals like leopards and lions, etc. Yet to my knowledge no Masai has ever held a Kenyan record in the javelin event, nor placed high in the national championships. This event has been dominated for years by a Kalenjin, Wilson Kiptalam, whose best was 233 feet, before John Mayaka, a Kisii , upped the record to 254'5½" in 1974.

There's an old adage that a soldier walks on his stomach. So it is true that a good athlete has to eat well. It's possible that the Kenyan diet, which consists mostly of natural, untampered foods, helps explain the success of the Kenyan runners. Except for a very few tribes, most notably the Masai who live almost solely on meat, milk and blood, the main meal for the rest of the Kenyans consists of foods high in natural (unrefined) carbohydrates. (*Editor:* What constitures a good diet is a matter of some dispute. The only general agreement among progressive nutritional scientists is that the better diets tend to be natural, i.e., not devitalized by refining, processing and excessive cooking. Thus, diets in lesser developed countries are usually superior to diets in technologically advanced countries because food isn't tampered with as much in the passage from the garden to the dinner table.)

The most common dish in Kenya is *ugali,* prepared by pounding maize flour in boiling water until the "grits" type of mixture becomes thick. The other main dish is *irio,* prepared by boiling maize (white corn; Kenyans have a strong dislike for North American yellow corn) with either beans, peas or any other seeds of the legume family. Some tribes will also add raw bananas, cassava and green vegetables like spinach, cabbage or carrots. African meals are mostly composed of one main dish and in the case of *irio* it is served for both lunch and the evening meal. But the *ugali* is always served with something else, like fish, meat stew, sour milk, beans or soup made from varied foods.

Fish is the main source of protein for the coastal tribes and those living around Lake Victoria in the west. The Kalenjin drink plenty of milk, but for the rest of the tribes, and especially those in the farming areas in central Kenya, beans, eggs and chicken are the main sources of protein. But this rigid division has been interrupted by urbanization, with *ugali* being supplemented by meat and milk in the cities, and the introduction of boarding high schools, where the meals served are almost uniform across the country: *irio, ugali* and rice supplemented mainly by meat stew.

AN ATHLETIC TRAINING PARADISE

But possibly, more than the diet, it is the geographical location and cultural surroundings which account for the development of athletic prowess among the Kenyans. Kenya, which straddles the Equator, can justifiably be called an athletic training paradise (except, of course, for winter sports). There are lakes and ocean for the water sportsmen, and plains and high-altitude training facilities for the runners. All are within reach for most would-be users, and are both available and ideally usable all year around. For the Kenyans, there is but one handicap: the lack of coaches.

The climate across the country is ideal for running. There is not a single day, even during the torrential tropical rains, when it is impossible to train outside—although most Kenyans will skip training when there is a drizzle, and would consider temperatures below 50 degrees F (which are very rare) too cold for training. The annual mean temperature varies with each geographical area. In the coastal areas, the mean temperature is higher and so is the humidity. For instance, in Mombasa, Kenya's biggest coastal city, the mean temperature is around 80°F, and maximums of over 90°F are common. However, training conditions for long distance runners are ideal on the (not yet polluted) beaches where cool breezes from the ocean make training not just comfortable but enjoyable. Long distance runners from up-country visiting the coast can double the daily training mileage without even noticing. Training away from the beach in the coastal areas, however, should be done either early in the morning or late in the evening to avoid the heat.

Nairobi, Kenya's administrative and commercial capital, with a population of approximately three-quarters of a million, has a mean temperature of 67.2°F. The coldest nights are 57° and noon temperatures are around 78. Other towns, Nyeri, Nanyuki, Eldoret and Nakuru, experience similar temperatures. Kisumu, on the shores of Lake Victoria, is slightly warmer.

The country is divided into eight administrative provinces—Coast, North Eastern, Central, Rift Valley, Nyanza, Western and Nairobi. Each province enters a team in the national track and field championships, with the Army entering a separate team. For the last decade, the Army team has dominated the championships, with the help of Kisii runners Charles Asati, Hezekiah Nyamau, Naftali Temu, and Kalenjin runners Wilson Kiprugut, Anthony Kipruto and Ben Kogo, to name but a few. Only Nairobi (the champion team in 1963) offers an occasional challenge, with the help of Kenya Prisons and Police athletes.

EARLY HABITS SHAPE FUTURE INTERESTS

Although the Masai, as mentioned earlier, have never done as well in the javelin as expected, it is evident that in Kenya early habits play a major role in shaping future interests in sport. There are numerous examples of this. Around the coast and Lake Victoria, the only toy known to young boys is a small tennis ball, which they kick around with such skill at an early age as to amaze the Brazilian soccer king, Pele. As might be expected, soccer, the Kenyan national sport (not track and field), is dominated by members of the Luo and Abaluhya tribes who live around Lake Victoria and in Western Province. There's also a sprinkling of players from the coast. Kenyans of Asian origin give their sons field hockey sticks for toys. In field hockey, another sport in which Kenya is highly rated (fifth in the world in 1971), 99% of the participants are Asians formerly from India.

In the case of the Kisii, one track fan jokingly remarked that Kisii boys do not know how to walk, they run even when it is inconvenient for them to do so, like when carrying an open bucket of water from a well. The Kalenjin, like most other pastoral tribes, must cover great distances whether going to elementary school (most high schools in Kenya are boarding schools), going to market or attending to their animals. The Kikuyus are said to be aggressive by nature; hence boxing is dominated by Kikuyus from Central Province, although recently other tribes, especially Luhya and Luo, have advanced into the ranks. Kamba, the tribe of the writer, excels in a non-Olympic but more sensual discipline—dancing.

A look at Kenya's contingent to the 1972 Olympics may help illustrate this tribal, but evidently natural, selection of the nation's flag-bearers to international competition. Members of the men's track and field team included: (Kisii)— Robert Ouko, John Mwebi, Charles Asati, Hezekiah Nyamau, Daniel Omwanza, Paul Mose, Richard Juma and Naftali Temu; (Kalenjin)—Julius Sang, William

Koskei, Mike Murei, Fatwell Kimaiyo, Thomas Saisi, Mike Boit, Cosmas Sielei, Ben Jipcho, Amos Biwott and Kipchoge Keino. Both girls on the track team, Tecla Chemabwai and Cherono Maiyo, were also Kalenjin. The only member of the team who wasn't a Kisii or Kalenjin was sprinter Dan Amuke (10.2 for 100 meters), a Teso from Western Province. In boxing, Kenya's eight-man Olympic team was made up of five Kikuyus, two Luhyas and a Teso. Silvester Ashioya was the lone black African selected to the field hockey team.

AN ABUNDANCE OF TALENT

It cannot be overstated that Kenya, and Africa for that matter, abounds with running talent. Strange as it may sound, it is possible that inside those mud huts today there are people who, if they had only continued competing, could have matched or even surpassed the Africans who have to date inscribed their names on the all-time lists.

There is evidence to suggest that John Akii-Bua's brothers, when training under similar conditions, were better than John himself. Mexico City 10,000-meter champion Naftali Temu once told me that his older brother was a better athlete than he, but the brother terminated his running career mainly because he was a member of the Seventh Day Adventist church, which forbids working (and running) on Saturday, their day of rest. Temu said that since most of the important competitions in the area were held on Saturdays, his brother never had the chance to continue competition.

Bruce Tulloh, the former British long distance star, spent two years as a teacher and part-time coach at Kenyatta College in Nairobi. Writing for a London daily, he once said, "Every Kenyan runner one meets talks of other better runners who used to beat him in races back in (elementary) school and local competitions."

What happens to those "other better runners"? Usually they leave the sport at a young age and are never seen on the track again. How good could they have become if they had continued? No one knows.

It wasn't until 1972 that Kenyan track was to witness the return and emergence of one of those "better" runners left in the village. The runner was Richard Juma and his success story unfolded right there in front of Tulloh (although Tulloh probably didn't know it) on that dusty Mombasa track at the 1972 Kenyan Championships.

"I used to beat Temu in the three miles in the Locational meetings in 1962," Juma had told me as we rode a Prison Services bus to Mombasa two days before the meet. Up to that time in the season, Juma had been the leading 10,000-meter runner in the country, but he had yet to qualify for the Olympics. His main opposition at the trials in Mombasa was going to be Temu, who, due to an achilles tendon injury two years earlier, had not been running well. Temu had been given a trip to Japan a month earlier, which most people thought should have been given to the then-fitter Juma. Only in low-altitude Mombasa or an overseas trips can Kenyans hope to qualify for major events like the Commonwealth or Olympic Games.

As is customary in many Kenyan meets, the 10,000-meter event was second to last at Mombasa. The cinder track, after two days pounding, was so loose as to resemble the sandy beaches a few blocks from the stadium. The two Kisii runners,

*Richard Juma was out of running for almost eight years but came back to be-
come Kenya's fastest-ever 10,000-meter runner. Here he leads the '74 Commonwealth Games 10,000 in which he set the Kenyan record of 27:57.0 in finishing
third to New Zealand's Dick Tayler (480) and England's Dave Black (238).
(Ed Lacey)*

Temu and Juma, exchanged the lead on every lap. The better-informed people
in the crowd fully expected Juma to drop Temu, but the determined Temu knew
otherwise. When the gun went for the final lap, Juma took an early lead around
the first bend, with Temu right on his shoulder. At the 200-meter mark Juma
kicked, but it was Temu's sprint that sent the stadium into an uproar. Guy Spen-
cer, then senior sports writer for the *East African Standard*, jumped out of his
seat and shouted excitedly, "Look! Look! Temu is back to form! Who said he
was finished?" as Temu streaked down the homestraight to break the tape in
28:21.4, the fastest time ever on African soil. The time would have been under
28 minutes on a Tartan track.

Juma qualified for the Olympics with 28:32.6, then the third best clocking
for the distance by a Kenyan. (Kip Keino held the Kenyan record at the time,
28:06.4, set in Russia). It wasn't until two years later that Juma finally put
his name in the Kenyan record book, when he ran 27:57.0 to take third spot in
the Commonwealth Games 10,000, beating, among others, Dave Bedford, the
world record holder at the distance.

The circumstances by which Richard Juma was able to return from an early retirement are rare. Most of the others never make it back. In Juma's case,
he had laid off competition for nearly eight years to fulfill his father's wish that
he should stop running, marry and bring up a family. This he did rather obedi-
ently. By 1969 he had four children. The eldest, a son, was later to give him motivation when, at age six, he was heard telling his age-group mates at a meet in

which Juma was running, "*Huyo in baba, atashinda, atashinda*" (Swahili for "That is dad, he will win, he will win.") Of course, Juma did not disappoint his son.

Juma was only able to resume running at age 25 mainly because he was an employee of the Kenya Prisons. At the time Jim Wambua, an enthusiastic young coach, had just returned from the US (where he had been going to school) and was putting together a strong, enthusiastic Prisons track squad. Wambua has since become Kenya's national coach. Another reason why Juma was able to come back is that he does not drink alcohol. This juice has claimed many would-be track greats in Kenya.

LATE MATURING

Kenyans mature late in comparison to their Western counterparts (and since most Kenyans do not continue their education past elementary school, most of the country's potential track stars are lost from the sport almost before they have a chance to get started). Kip Keino could only run 5:49 for the mile at age 16. At 24, the best he could do was 4:20. He finally hit stardom in '65 at age 26, after 10 years of competition, when he ran 3:54.2 for the mile and set world records in the 3000 and 5000 meters.

Ben Jipcho was 30 and had been running for 11 years when he finally reached the top in 1973, setting the current 3000-meter steeplechase record of 8:14 and achieving the number one ranking in the world in both the steeplechase and the mile/1500. Behind his success, there was a great deal of hard work. Unlike most of his fellow Kenyan distance runners, Jipcho has to supplement his great talents with corresponding amounts of work. If he doesn't train hard, he tends to gain weight. Of course, like other athletes in the services (Jipcho was an officer in the Kenya Prisons Department), he had sufficient time to train, a priviledge not available to other athletes working with private firms or attending Nairobi University.

Recently, some private firms, realizing the publicity to be had from having a star runner such as Jipcho or Keino on their payroll, have remarkably followed the example of the national services in allowing athletes time to train. But Nairobi University, like other universities throughout Africa, still treats sport strictly as leisure, spare-time activities. As well, degrees in Physical Education, at this early stage of East African development, are a luxury that can ill be afforded. There are other pressing needs to be met by the few souls who make it through the sparsely peopled corridors of an African university. The list of former Kenyan secondary schools' national champions who have never continued in track and field after enrolling at Nairobi University is impressive.

Kenyatta College, which recently became a branch of Nairobi University, does offer PE courses but these are far below par with those offered at US or British universities. Kenya today remains hard pressed for qualified PE teachers in its secondary schools. Such posts are currently filled by foreigners who are rarely qualified in physical education (ie., their speciality is usually one or more of the other teaching subjects).

However, it is to such "unqualified" British track and field coaches, along with others who have had a relatively sound coaching background, that much of the credit for Kenya's track success must go. High school headmasters like Curry Francis and later Larry Campbell at Alliance High School, and Catholic Brother

Simion at St. Patrick's High School, Iten, have raised to stardom such schools' champions as Mike Boit and Mike Murei, while others like history teacher Mike Bailey at Machakos (and later at Kenyatta College) were able to field a Kenyan secondary schools' championship team by the simple trick of showing up at the training ground with a stopwatch as the A-Z tool. Now Africans with similar backgrounds, like Mumbuni Day Secondary School Headmaster Daniel Mulwa, are able to put together a national secondary schools' cross-country championship team (in 1973). Yes, the spirit has caught up.

The people, however, who laid the foundation for Kenyan track, were qualified British coaches, mainly from two famous PE schools, Loughborough and Carnegie. These coaches undertook ambitious projects, some using tree branches for javelins and, of course, bamboo for vaulting poles. They had the athletes to work with, but almost no facilities. No wonder Kenyans were still running barefooted as late as the 1964 Olympics (Temu, for instance, in the 10,000). Even today, Kenya, and to a great extent Africa as a whole, is almost a decade behind in facilities and coaching in the field events. Of course, the natural talent is there.

It was the enthusiastic brothers Archie and Eddie Evans who supplied the early inspiration in Kenya. Archie, as the first Kenya national sports officer, coached Kenyan teams at several international meets in the '50s. Eddie Evans and his wife Ann have been in Kenya for nearly 20 years combining a coaching and teaching career unparalleled by any other couple in the country. At Siriba College, Eddie Evans organized numerous cross-country races, which are today the basis for the success of Kenya distance runners. Eddie moved to Kenyatta College in 1965 and brought with him from Siriba another dedicated Britisher, Alex Stewart, whose computer-style organization of cross-country meets has won him country-wide praise. Stewart was mainly responsible for Mike Boit's breakthrough into international ranking in 1972.

THE CONTROVERSIAL JOHN VELZIAN

Probably the best known Kenyan coach internationally is the controversial Englishman John Velzian, whose habitual use of the pronoun "I" cost him what would otherwise have been a glamorous career as Kenya's national coach. Velzian, a graduate of Carnegie College, coached Kenya's national teams which were highly successful in the first All-African Games in Brazzaville, the Congo, in 1965 and the British Commonwealth Games in Kingston, Jamaica in 1966. But his conflict with the Kenya AAA officials cost him his post before the '68 Mexico City Olympics.

Velzian undoubtedly ranks among the top four qualified coaches in Kenya, along with Charles Mukora, Bob Hancock and Jim Wambua, but he is not superior as he's otherwise been credited. Unlike the case with the other three coaches mentioned, I have yet to meet a Kenyan champion athlete who gives Velzian sole credit for his/her success.

Probably the most knowledgeable of the foreign coaches in Kenya, and probably the best, has been Bob Hancock, a math teacher at Bishop Otunga High School in Kisii land. Among others, Hancock has coached Robert Ouko, Paul Mose and Patrick Onyango. (*Editor:* Hancock has since left Kenya and is now teaching back in Britain.)

Among the native Kenyan coaches, former national coach Charles Mukora, who coached Kenyan teams at Mexico City, Edinburgh and Munich, and his successor, Jim Wambua, assistant coach in Munich and the head coach at the '74 Commonwealth Games in Christchurch, New Zealand, stand out. Mukora's personality has won him respect from both athletes and officials. He has sound judgment, and reacts suitably in demanding situations. His biggest weakness is that he only coaches during the big meets and is rarely seen helping athletes with their daily training, even in Nairobi where he lives. Wambua, on the other hand, is more enthusiastic. He associates with athletes at all levels, shows great understanding for athletes' problems on and off the track and, unlike the rest, who all have British coaching background or training, he is US educated.

Other coaches who have contributed significantly to Kenyan track and field are John Ndungu, former games tutor at Nairobi University, Hussein Ali, games tutor at Kenya Sciences Teachers' College, and retired international athletes Wilson Kiprugut (in the Army) and Kimaru Songok (in the Police). Among the women, only Yasmin Ismail has shown dedication on a par with the male coaches.

AN ANSWER TO THE COACHING PROBLEMS?

In April 1972, most of the aforementioned coaches conducted a week-long coaching clinic, a brain child of the then Kenyan Amateur Athletic Association secretary Feisal Sherman. This clinic was the first of its kind in Kenya. More such clinics could be one of the answers to Kenya's coaching problems. Maybe through sharing coaching experience, Kenya can come up with a super coach to train the super athletes. Such a coach would have the personality of Mukora, the superior psychological motivation of Velzian, the expertise of Hancock and the drive and enthusiasm of Wambua.

Kenya's coaching situation will no doubt be much improved when the majority of Kenyan athletes currently studying in American universities, most of them PE majors, return to Kenya after graduation.

The body which runs track and field in Kenya, the Kenya Amateur Athletic Association, was founded in 1950. Its first president, the wealthy Sir Derek Erskine, who had to bow out to the demand of "Africanization" in 1965, is one of the founding members still dedicated to the sport in Kenya. Since 1965, the KAAA has been headed by former Kenyan track internationals, the current president being Charles Mukora.

Under former president Musembi Mbathi, who succeeded Sir Derek, the organization started projects to promote competition among the young. With financial support from a tobacco and tea company, the association runs up to seven meetings at different venues per year. In addition, the administrative structure makes possible annual competitions, starting at the location, division, district levels and culminating with the interprovincial championships (i.e. the National Championships). The best two in each event at the latter competition win a place on the Kenyan team to the East Africa Championships.

However, the birth of the Kenya Secondary Schools national championships in 1966 took much of the glamor away from the national body. The schools' championship was a dream of Aish Jeneby, then Physical Education Inspector of Schools and long-time secretary of the KAAA. The competition was set up under the guidance of John Velzian. It is to the schools' championships that Kenya has come to look for its future champions. With the exception of a few athletes from the national services, the majority of the Kenyan team is now composed of former schools' champions. Unlike the Keino, Temu, Kogo generation, younger runners like Ben Jipcho, Julius Sang, Robert Ouko, Mike Boit and John Ngeno are all past schools' champions. The schools' competition is organized along similar lines as the KAAA meets (i.e., regional meets culminating in a national championship), and it is undoubtedly here that the future of Kenyan track and field will be determined.

In Zambia, A Different Picture
by Ross Kidd

While countries like Kenya, Ethiopia, and more recently, Uganda and Tanzania, have won world fame in track, many other African countries, like Tanzania's neighbor Zambia, haven't come close to making a mark on the world track scene. At the 1972 Olympics, for instance, Zambia had only two entrants in the track events: Benson Mulomba, who ran 1:53.4 to finish fifth in his heat of the 800 meters; and Ngwila Musonda, who ran 14:37.4 to finish 13th and last in his heat of the 5000 meters.

Why Zambia struggles along in the ranks of the Have-Nots of African track (when it apparently has tremendous natural talent in the running events) is the subject of this article. We include it here to lend perspective to the African track picture.

Ross Kidd is a 29-year old Canadian who formerly worked in Zambia with the the Canadian University Services Overseas (CUSO). He is now in Francistown, Botswana where he is director of an extra-mural services office of the University of Botswana, Lesotho and Swaziland. A competitive distance runner for the past 15 years, he is the younger brother of Bruce Kidd, Canada's sensational teenage runner of the early '60s (gold medallist—at age 19!—in the six miles at the '62 Commonwealth Games).

I worked in Zambia from 1966 to 1969 and was very active in athletics— actually editing a "semi-occasional" athletic journal. The main aim of the magazine was to make Zambian athletes more performance conscious. As I wrote in 1967: "If Zambians are to become more proficient in this sport whose by-law is the stopwatch, they must learn the significance of time and pace-judgment. It is only when one becomes aware of relative times that the significance of certain performances becomes evident and improvement can be recognized. The ironic situation where the Zambian mile record holder does not know whether his best mile is four minutes or five minutes must be changed."

Zambia's potential in track and field lies in middle and long distance running. Zambians are naturals for these events, having developed strength and endurance through force of circumstance. It is not uncommon to see Zambians running to work. Once during a workout along Lusaka's Independence Avenue, I ran for a long time beside a house servant running to buy a newspaper for his boss.

But to develop a Zambian "Keino" or "Jipcho", Zambian runners must shake off the impression of the Kenyan athletes as "gods" endowed with a unique, mystical gift for running. They must see that Keino, Jipcho and company are "mortals", simply dedicated athletes with miles and miles of hard training behind them. When Zambian runners recognize this, their aspirations for international track prowess will not seem so hopeless. At the same time they will see the tough, self-sacrificing struggle that lies ahead of them before they reach their goal.

Regular, systematic and long-term training has yet to be accepted even by top-class athletes in Zambia. Most athletes train for short periods of the year during the competitive season but then take long periods of rest. For distance runners this means there is no progressive development over a long time.

The Zambian attitude towards training is hard to fight. Zambians would prefer to keep sport *fun* and *competitive*. In soccer they prefer to go out and have a game rather than spend the time developing the individual skills required for soccer. Similarly in track and field, the athletes would prefer to run the full distance at top speed rather than do overdistance work or interval training.

In his book *A Clean Pair Of Heels*, the great New Zealand runner Murray Halberg described an interval training clinic he and Gordon Pirie ran for the natives on the Zambian Copperbelt before Independence. Said Halberg, "Their idea of athletic training was beyond us. We tried to give them some indication of running and pace judgment. We tried to explain how to train without racing, but it was hopeless. I told one group we would try to run 220 yards in 30 seconds to show them the speed they should run at in training to be good milers. Away we went and I ran my 30 seconds spot on. But 49 laughing Africans were in front of me. The slowest was 30 yards in front. They just refused to jog around and regarded every run as a race."

In Zambia it is very difficult to impart the view that training involves disciplined and systematic preparation for a competition six months away. Instead one must introduce short-term goals and keep training fun. Major improvements will come when athletes begin to enjoy their training and find regular competition to sustain their training buildup over long periods.

A CHICKEN-AND-EGG DILEMMA

It is a truism to say that a strong national track and field team is based on a broad base of athletes and competition. In Zambia I found it to be the usual chicken-and-egg dilemma. There were not enough athletes to sustain regular competitions and vice-versa. There are various league matches arranged, but one finds oneself competing against the same people time and time again. It's not very stimulating.

Travel difficulties also restrict competition. Transportation along the line-of-rail between Lusaka, the capital, and the Copperbelt present no major problems; however, in the rural area it becomes difficult. A friend in Barotse province once wrote me: "Kalabo (name of an athlete) took 36 hours by barge down the Zambesi to return from the athletics meeting. . . For another

track meet, 50 of us on the back of the five-ton truck in blazing heat took five
hours to cover the 68 miles to Senanga. What a journey, but what tremendous
value to our competitors and to the 1000 entertainment-starved spectators
who watched the competition at the tiny Boma!"

Transportation not only restricts competition within Zambia, but also on the
international scene. With Rhodesia out of the picture due to its political and
racial policy, the closest competitors in Dar es Salaam are over 1000 miles away
along the formidable Hell Run to Tanzania (the petrol lorry route).

The parochial attitudes of Zambian officials have intensified this isolation.
They tend to regard their local programs as the be-all and end-all of athletics
and create few opportunities for their runners outside the border.

In 1966 when I first arrived in Zambia there were only *30* competitors in the national championship meet!—partly due to a gasoline shortage
which made travel even more difficult than normally. After 1966 the Zambian
Amateur Athletic Association tried to hold the national championships in
a different region each year in order to stimulate interest within each region,
but this had no long-term effect.

A peripatetic coaching scheme was tried, but this also proved a failure
since the visits were so brief and very little could be communicated in such a
short time. In the '60s the United States sponsored a peripatetic coaching
scheme in Africa built around former Olympic great Mal Whitfield, but this
was always poorly organized in my experience. Mal would arrive for a one-week
clinic that would be publicized at the last moment by the US Information
Service without any official communication with the ZAAA. The clinic would
consist of a highly structured lecture and demonstration with very little
opportunity for participants to express their areas of interests or to ask questions.
The goals of the clinic or what participants were expected (coaches, athletes, administrators) was never clearly stated, and so a group with very mixed backgrounds
and interests always turned out. This type of clinic only seemed to work well
where the national team had already been selected and needed some help in preparing for an international competition.

Improvement will only come when trained Zambian sports directors
are assigned to secondary schools and other major institutions. Training
courses for coaches to date have been sporadic and *ad hoc* and largely
restricted to soccer. There are few track coaches and most have had no
training. A few Zambians have attended training courses overseas but most of
these Zambians have found more lucrative employment outside sports administration and coaching. The rural isolation and low-paying jobs in Zambian secondary
schools (the logical base for a national athletics movement) have attracted very
few Zambian graduates and as a result these schools still have 80% expatriate
staff. The turn-over of expatriate staff is chronic and militates against any
continuity in sports development at a school.

Outside the major institutions (schools, Army, Polic ', there is virtually
no track and field. The track club in the capital city is the only one in
Zambia not based on a major supporting institution. (Clubs in the Copperbelt
are run by full-time sport workers in the welfare department of the mines.)
As a result, most school-leavers or those who leave the Army or Police
abandon track and field altogether. It is again the chicken-or-egg

dilemma: do they abandon track and field because of lack of opportunity (in the form of clubs), or are clubs not formed since school-leavers as adults are no longer interested in active participation in sport?

Whatever the answer, an obvious strategy would be to concentrate one's resources on three major institutions—schools, Police and Army. All three institutions have an active track and field program, but it is restricted to a particular season of the year, and then displaced from attention by other sports. Performances could improve if these institutions began to accept the notion that track and field should be a year-round activity and developed specialist coaches for this sport.

STIFF COMPETITION FROM SOCCER

Track and field also faces stiff, and one might say unfair, competition from soccer, the national sport. Soccer is the glamor sport in Zambia. It receives more publicity and has far more resources than track. The government—through its Sports Directorate—could help to improve track and field by channelling some of the resources and attention from soccer into track.

When I was in Zambia I held the dubious distinction of being the fastest white runner in the country, with times likes 4:45 (mile), 15:30 (three miles) and 32:05 (six miles) at Lusaka's 5000-foot altitude. But being the best white runner meant nothing. You could count on the fingers of one hand the number of Europeans who compete in long distance races in Zambia. Besides, the Zambians were streets ahead. The potential of the Zambian athletes in middle and long distance running amazed me. They can train once a year and come out and beat you. With a little bit of coaching, more training and incentives to train hard, they'd have no difficulty holding their own against the Keinos, Jipchos, Gammoudis, etc. In the field events, of course, the potential is not as evident. The Zambian is a natural runner, but not a technique man. It will take a tremendous amount of coaching before a 15-foot pole vaulter, a 60-foot shot putter, or a 200-foot javelin thrower emerges.

Perhaps what Zambia needs most is a national star in track. As I wrote in 1967: (My) brother Bruce and Bill Crothers in Canada, Keino in Kenya, and Bikila in Ethiopia were responsible for a surge of interest in track in their respective countries. Such Zambian soccer stars as "Zoom" Ndhlovu and "King" Muhango have had a tremendous impact on the youth of Zambia. With one or two runners of international caliber, some of the enthusiasm could be swung from soccer to track."

Chapter Six

African Recruiting Boom

by John Manners

One of the results of the African success in track and field in the last decade has been the tremendous increase in the recruiting of African athletes by US universities. As of the 1974-75 school year, there were more than 50 African athletes on track scholarships in the US. As John Manners reports here, some strong nationalistic opposition to this recruiting boom has been voiced in both Africa and the US.

A banner headline on the lead sports page of the Nairobi, Kenya, *Daily Nation* in December 1974 read: "Leave Our Athletes Alone." The story that followed was an interview with Kenya's national track coach, Jim Wambua. "I feel Kenya is being exploited by Americans," Wambua was quoted as saying. "They are out to get hold of our potential stars to boost standards at their universities . . .It is time something was done to put a stop to it."

Though it might come as a surprise to Wambua, his position is supported, albeit indirectly, by a number of coaches at American universities. Mel Brodt of Bowling Green State University, president of the US Track and Field Coaches Association, is an outspoken opponent of the recruiting of foreign athletes. "What are our institutions for?" asks Brodt. "Are they to enhance the ready-made foreign athlete, or are they to develop our own American athlete?"

But for all this nationalistic opposition on both sides, foreign recruiting by US colleges is booming, particularly in track, and the richest new vein in the overseas talent mine is Africa. From Kenya alone, 12 new recruits arrived to take up track scholarships during the 1974-75 academic year, bringing the overall total to more than 50 Africans on track scholarships at US colleges, plus perhaps a few dozen others who came to America under other auspices and now compete in track and field for their schools.

AN IMPACT OUT OF PROPORTION TO NUMBERS

What's more, the impact of these African athletes on intercollegiate competition is totally out of proportion to their numbers. There were only 12 Africans out of over 600 competitors at the 1974 NCAA outdoor championships, but of those 12, nine made the finals in their respective events and seven of them scored, accounting for a total of 43 points. Earlier in the year at the NCAA indoor championships, Africans won three of the 15 individual events and placed second in two others. At the NAIA outdoor championships, Africans won six events and accounted for 61 of the 67 points that won the meet for Eastern New Mexico University.

These results are perhaps not surprising in light of the fact that a number of the African athletes at American colleges are seasoned international competitors. George Daniels and Ohene Karikari, both formerly of Colorado, Josh Owusu and Kofi Okyir of Angelo State, and Moise Pomaney of Howard Paine have all won medals for Ghana at the Commonwealth Games; Julius Sang and Robert Ouko of North Carolina Central, and Mike Boit of Eastern New Mexico have each won Olympic medals for Kenya.

Competitive records like these are what US coaches who oppose foreign recruiting point to most often. Jim Bush, track coach at UCLA, complained at the 1974 NCAA championships that his relay squad would have to beat "the Kenya Olympic team" (i.e., Sang and Ouko) in order to win their own national championship. On the other hand Dr. Leroy Walker, who brought Sang and Ouko to North Carolina Central, argues in favor of foreign participation. "The NCAA's are the *collegiate* championships," says Walker. "Any bona fide student in the university ought to be able to participate. Robert Ouko and Julius Sang are honor students at North Carolina Central. They're an important part of our student body, and they qualify for every activity a student is allowed to engage in."

Dr. Walker's argument notwithstanding, the two Kenyans were banned from the 1972 and '73 NCAA championships under an NCAA by-law which was generally known as the "overage-foreigner rule." Passed in 1961, the rule was directed against what were regarded as abuses in foreign recruiting in soccer, tennis and hockey, as well as track. It stated essentially that for every year a foreign athlete competed abroad after his 20th birthday (later changed to 19th), he would lose a year of varsity eligibliity for NCAA championship competition. The rule was quickly adopted by most of the major athletic conferences, so it soon applied to most intercollegiate competition, not just NCAA championships.

When Ouko and Sang arrived in Durham to enroll at North Carolina Central in the fall of 1971, they were both in their mid-20s. Dr. Walker had been trying to get them to NCCU since he first met them at the Mexico City Olympics in 1968. He iced the deal on a visit to Kenya in 1971 while he was busy organizing the first US-Africa track meet, to be held in Durham. He visited both runners at home, convinced them that NCCU was the place for them, and helped to get them leaves of absence from their duties in the Kenya Prisons Service. He had hoped to recruit Ben Jipcho and Amos Biwott at the same time, but they had other commitments.

Nevertheless, Walker was pleased with the two Kenyans who did come to NCCU. Ouko was the 1970 Commonwealth 800-meter champion, and both he and Sang had gold medals from Kenya's Commonwealth Games winning 1600-meter relay team. In their first outdoor season in America, the two Kenyans performed spectacularly at a couple of big invitational meets and contributed to a world and a collegiate relay record. They were all set to take the NCAA by storm when they were reminded of the overage-foreigner rule.

The rule had all but stopped the recruiting of Africans before it ever really got under way. In the 1960s, the early years of independence of most African countries, athletes who were worth recruiting, who spoke fluent English, who had finished secondary school, and who could manage to take college board exams were rare enough. But in countries where most kids start school at age 10 or 11, if at all, athletes who could meet these requirements before turning 20 were practically non-existent.

THE FIRST AFRICANS

A few, however, did find their way to American colleges, particularly in the Ivy League. In the early '60s, Harvard came up with Chris Ohiri, the center forward of the Nigerian national soccer team, who was a 50-foot triple jumper in the off-season, and Aggrey Awori, a two-time Olympian from Uganda and African record holder in the high hurdles. Cornell, through the good offices of a Kenyan alumnus, picked up distance runner Steve Machooka, who became IC4A cross-country champion as a sophomore and was undefeated in individual competition until he ran into academic eligibility problems. In the mid-60's, Yale's track fortunes were boosted by Ohene Frempong, Ghanaian national record holder in the high hurdles, who eventually gave up running in favor of medical studies.

By the late '60s, a few schools like Villanova, Brigham Young and the University of Texas at El Paso were winning meets with the aid of corps of foreign athletes. Their coaches usually made sure that these aliens could prove they were young enough to get their full quota of NCAA eligibility. Most of them came from Britain, Ireland, Scandinavia, Australia and the Caribbean. Any Africans competing in track for American colleges at this point were generally at small NAIA schools not affected by NCAA age restrictions.

Then, in the fall of 1970, two international-caliber African athletes arrived on track scholarships at big NCAA schools: Ghanaian sprinter George Daniels at Colorado and Kenyan triple jumper Patrick Onyango at Wisconsin. Both had been recruited the previous year by two well-known American athletes—Bill Toomey and Mark Winzenried—during the course of a US Information Service tour of Africa.. Toomey recruited Daniels for his alma mater, and Winzenried, still a student at Wisconsin, got Onyango to join him there.

Despite fine performances by Daniels and Onyango, coaches at other NCAA schools remained cautious, and only a few more Africans arrived the next year. With the aid of Daniels and a Peace Corps volunteer in Accra, Colorado recruited two more Ghanaians, long jumper Kingsley Adams and triple jumper James Nyumutei. At about the same time, Ouko and Sang arrived at North Carolina Central. The two Kenyans attracted so much attention with their performances for NCCU and later that year at the Olympics, that even after Ouko and Sang were barred from the NCAA Championships, coaches around the country began scrambling to establish "African connections."

Once again, schools in the NAIA, with no age restrictions to worry about, were generally quicker to go after the Africans. In the fall of 1972, Eastern New Mexico picked up a Kenyan hurdler named Tom Esikhati, originally recruited by an NCAA school, Washington State, but dropped by them because he was too old for four years of NCAA eligibility. By the following January, with Esikhati's help, Eastern New Mexico had enrolled two more Kenyans, international distance runner Philip Ndoo and Olympic 800-meter medallist Mike Boit.

TWO FOR THE PRICE OF A STAMP

Meanwhile, Washington State established a Kenyan connection of their own. A Kenyan who taught at the University of Puget Sound contacted John Chaplin, then assistant coach at Washington State. He told Chaplin he had a brother back in Kenya who was a 14-second high hurdler, and his brother had a friend who was a world class distance runner. Chaplin was skeptical, but he wrote to the two athletes. Almost as if by return mail came John Kiplangat Ngeno, soon to become Pacific-8 high hurdles champion, and John Kipkemoi Ngeno (no relation), who became a multiple NCAA distance titlist and, by 1974, one of the world's greatest 10,000-meter runners. "It was the easiest recruiting I've ever done," says Chaplin.

By the end of 1973, still more coaches had become believers, and a change was on the way that would make African recruiting even easier. Earlier that year the NCAA had stripped Howard University in Washington, D.C., of its 1971 national soccer title, partly on the grounds that several of Howard's players had been overage foreigners. Howard took the NCAA to court, challenging the constitutionality of the rule. On Dec. 10, 1973, a federal court ordered the rule suspended because it failed to comply with the equal protection clause of the 14th Amendment.

The court ruling was a boon to all foreign recruiting, but its greatest effect was on the formerly "overage" Africans. One of the coaches to take fullest advantage of the ruling was Ted Banks of the University of Texas at El Paso. In December 1973, Banks had a Kenyan and two Ghanaians on his squad, all freshmen whom he had contacted through their compatriots at Eastern New Mexico and Colorado. Just over a year later there were nine Africans competing for UTEP, and talk of more on the way. "Once you get one," says Banks, "you've got a foot in the door." Banks has his feet in a number of doors, with athletes from Canada, Australia, Ireland, Sweden and India, as well as Kenya and Ghana, on his team, but his most effective sales pitch has been aimed at the Africans.

Banks feels he can make best use of his limited recruiting funds by spending them on what he calls "proven athletes". Foreign athletes who are talented enough to attract the attention of American coaches tend to be more experienced than American high school graduates, and they usually become more serious students as well. But best of all, from Bank's point of view, they're easier to recruit. "I just have to write a few letters and make a few phone calls," says Banks. "The competition for American athletes is intense, and we're way off in the desert where we can't impress the student with our facilities or our campus. I mean. you bring a Los Angeles kid to El Paso and he's not going to appreciate what the place has to offer."

AFRICANS MORE APPRECIATIVE

Foreign athletes, on the other hand, are most appreciative. Africans in particular are so eager for a chance at an American degree that they wouldn't think

of asking for the kinds of privileges and "extras" (apartments, cars) commonly demanded by American athletes of comparable promise. So the overage-foreigner rule was not the only reason that so many talented Africans have found themselves at small, out of the way schools like Howard Payne, Angelo State, North Carolina Central and Eastern New Mexico. Bigger schools could afford to recruit Americans.

Outstanding African athletes who find themselves at small schools are often obliged to do more than their share at meets. Ghanaian Olympian Josh Owusu once won three individual events, took second in another and ran both relays for Angelo State at their conference championships. Kenyan Philip Ndoo has been known to run as many as 12 miles for Eastern New Mexico in a single meet, often after having driven 700 miles to get there. Ndoo says he enjoys the running, and he's philosophical about the problems posed by small school budgets. "For me," he says of Eastern New Mexico, "this place is all right. I've gone through harder times and I wasn't expecting heaven, especially in going to a small school. If I was going to UCLA or someplace like that I would expect to be treated like they treat people there, but here you would be pressing them too hard."

Another Kenyan recruited by Eastern New Mexico, Olympic 400-meter hurdler Mike Murei, was less ready to indulge the small budget shortcomings of the school, especially after he had heard about the comparitively luxurious circumstances his friend and countryman Mark Sang was enjoying at the University of Wisconsin. After a term at Eastern New Mexico, Murei transferred to the greener pastures of the Madison campus.

One of the reasons Murei gave for his leaving Eastern New Mexico was that he felt his presence there was partly responsible for his countryman, Tom Esikhati, losing his scholarship. Esikati was the first Kenyan on the campus, and he helped to recruit those who followed, but, ironically, as the performance standards on the track squad rose, the number of track scholarships was cut almost in half. Strictly on the basis of points won, Esikhati didn't qualify for aid, so he stopped running and began paying his own way with the help of his coach, who found a few financial corners for him to cut.

Another of the early African recruits, George Daniels, lost his scholarship at Colorado, but for different reasons. He arrived at Colorado in 1970 expecting to compete for four years and graduate, but under the overage-foreigner rule then in force, Daniels was declared ineligible after two years. His coach helped him to transfer to Illinois State, which belonged to a conference that didn't observe the rule. But once there, Daniels and two Nigerian friends got involved in a dispute with the coach and stopped competing. Daniels lost his scholarship, dropped out of school, and eventually came back when a new coach was appointed.

Africans recruited more recently have had difficulties of a different sort. Generally younger than their predecessors, and with less travel and competitive experience behind them, they have to adjust to more than simply their new athletic and academic circumstances. Wesley Maiyo, a young Kenyan half-miler,

John Ngeno, here leading the University of Oregon's Paul Geis in a collegiate dual meet, represented Kenya in the '70 Commonwealth Games at age 18! But it's since coming to Washington State University that he's risen to world ranking (third in the world in '74 for 10,000 meters). (Jeff Johnson photo)

left his home to enroll in the University of Wyoming in January 1974. He had
never flown before, never been outside his country, never seen snow or ice. He
found himself in the middle of a bitter Laramie winter with what he described as
"clothing appropriate to Kenya." He also found himself in the middle of a bitter
dispute between his white coach and a number of newly recruited black sprinters
and hurdlers from Washington, D.C., over alleged broken recruiting promises.

Maiyo's talent was such that even though he had never run indoors before
January, and had no proper indoor training facility at Wyoming, he won the
1000 yards at the NCAA indoor championships in March. But by June, his inad-
vertant involvement in the dispute between the coach and the black athletes re-
sulted in his missing the outdoor NCAA. By Christmas vacation, he was ready to
transfer, and had even registered at a junior college on the West Coast, when
threats by his former coach to protest alleged violations of NCAA transfer regu-
lations and even to call in Immigration Department officials to check imagined
visa violations brought Maiyo back to Wyoming.

ONE ATHLETE'S FRANK ASSESSMENT

Not surprisingly, some of the African athletes at American colleges view
their experiences with mixed feelings. Robert Ouko of Kenya and North Carolina
Central is one of the most outspoken. "It wouldn't be going too far to say that
in many cases African athletes are being exploited by American colleges," says
Ouko, "and getting precious little in return." Ouko feels that if an athlete is to
find time for his education in between track meets, he has to be able to resist
pressure from coaches and administrators who want him to spend all his time
training and competing. American students are aware of their rights and obliga-
tions, but, says Ouko, "Africans are afraid to stand up for themselves, afraid that
they will be thrown out and made to go home if they don't turn out as often as
they're told."

Ouko himself did manage to find the time he needed for study, but he
adds, "I had to fight for it against the American system of college education,
which puts sports on an absurdly high plane." Both Ouko and his classmate and
countryman, Julius Sang, did well enough at NCCU to be admitted to graduate
schools, though neither of them had even qualified for pre-university training in
Kenya before they left for the US in '71.

"Don't get me wrong," says Ouko, "I'm grateful for the chance to go to
the States and to get a higher education." Sang is grateful, too. After the remarks of the Kenya national coach attacking American university recruiting had
appeared in the Nairobi papers, Sang wrote a response. He argued that if African
athletes could get the same educational and training opportunities at home,
they'd stay home, but since there were no track scholarships in Africa, the athletes should take the opportunity to use their running talents to further their education.

Both Sang and Ouko suggest that a talented African athlete would be
smart not to leap at the first scholarship offer, since, given the boom in African
recruiting, more may follow. He should try to make sure that the school he
chooses is going to take the same pains to see that he graduates that it takes to
see that he competes.

As for the "track drain" in the African countries, in spite of the complaints
of Kenya national coach Jim Wambua and other African track officials, it can be

argued that African talent is being developed by American universities to the ultimate detriment of the United States and the benefit of African countries at the Olympic Games. This is precisely the position of the American opponents of foreign recruiting, who agree with Wambua that the movement of foreign athletes to American campuses should be stopped.

Kenya sports writer Norman Da Costa responded to Wambua's remarks, saying, "Young Kenyans on track scholarships in the United States gain immeasurably through competition with the best of American runners. If they were at home, they would stagnate for lack of competition. Besides, there is a lot of untapped athletic talent all round the country which our team selectors and talent scouts would do well to discover."

Ouko believes that Wambua, despite having had several years of US education himself, doesn't understand the way college sports work in America. Also, says Ouko, "He's concerned because he's losing the glory that is earned by the athletes in America. He can't take any credit for their achievements." Some officials in Kenya speculate privately that the grumbling over the "track drain" may be due in part to a tribal imbalance in the number of Kenyan athletes in the United States. There are, for instance, practically no Kisii or Kamba athletes among the scholarship holders.

But regardless of what is being said in their home countries, and no matter how many difficulties they've had to put up with in America, African athletes at US colleges seem to feel that their American experience is, on balance, a positive thing. "I don't know any who regret having come," says Philip Ndoo. Perhaps when their improved talents are eventually repatriated, athletic officials in their own countries will feel the same way.

Chapter Seven

In the End, the Individual is the Key

by Dave Prokop

The author, who edited this book, is the assistant editor of Runner's World and a long-time runner. A Canadian now living in California, he is the meet director of the world-class Springbank International Road Races in London, Ontario.

In trying to understand why the African athletes, as a group, have been so successful in running, it's only natural to look for general explanations. This, in fact, is one of the things we have tried to do in this book. But in looking for such explanations it is all too easy to overlook the most important single factor of all in the African success story—individual human effort.

The importance of the human factor becomes readily apparent when one realizes there are, after all, thousands of people living in the areas that, for instance, Kip Keino and Ben Jipcho come from. Presumably, some of these people have as much natural talent as these two world famous runners (hasn't Keino, in fact, often said that there are many in Kenya with far greater natural talent for running than he has?). Yet there is only one Kip Keino, only one Ben Jipcho.

In the process of editing this book, I had occasion to talk with Billy Wandera, who is a graduate of the University of Nairobi and is now completing his graduate studies in engineering at Stanford University in California. Billy is not a runner, nor does he particularly follow track and field (although he is well aware, of course, of the exploits of his countrymen in the sport). A perceptive, thoughtful young man, he has some interesting things to say about Kenyan achievements and the reaction of the Western world to them.

"I get the impression," he says, "that the Western world is amazed at the ability of these athletes because it seems to have happened so suddenly. But I don't really think it is sudden. Before the 1950s, there were few opportunities to compete. The ability was always there.

"This amazement is not restricted to sports alone, by the way. In colonial days, many Africans were not given good educational opportunities and it was thought that they couldn't do certain things. Now that they are given the opportunity and show that they can do these things, people are amazed.

"I think the success of the Kenyan runners can be explained by looking at athletes in general throughout the world. What facts are common to all good runners in the world? To me, that is more important than looking at the cultural factors and so on.

"But in so much that is written to explain the success of these runners, there's hardly any mention of the competitive spirit of the athlete. Why don't more of these writers examine the individual athletes as people who like to compete, who like to succeed, who like to be noticed?"

It's probably safe to say that no one ever became an international champion in track and field without having a significant amount of natural talent. But no one ever became a champion in the sport—at least in the middle and long distance events—on natural talent alone. Over the last decade I have had the opportunity of interviewing numerous champion runners. I have yet to meet one who attributes his/her success solely or *even primarily* to natural talent, or who would not be insulted if someone else did. Yet, in one way or another, subtly and sometimes not so subtly, the world has been insulting the runners of Africa ever since Abebe Bikila in precisely this manner.

Of course, with all due respect to the African athletes, they themselves brought it about—by being too successful, too extraordinary, sometimes (seemingly) too super-human. And Bikila, the first in the long line of these remarkable runners, appeared the most super-human of them all. His unexpected, barefoot victory in Rome (have you ever tried running even one block barefooted at race pace!) and his astounding performance in Tokyo four years later, where he won by more than four minutes and then calmly did calisthenics on the infield, were not the sort of achievements, it seemed, that mere training or will-power could explain. Therefore, it was natural to see his victories in terms of some God-given ability (or altitude advantage) rather than in terms of hard training and perseverence.

But Abebe Bikila was no man-god. He did not become a great runner at the wave of some magician's wand. Onni Niskanen, Bikila's coach, told *Sports Illustrated* reporter John Underwood in 1965: "Before 1959, I hardly knew who this Abebe was. He ran only third in the marathon trial for the Rome Olympics and already then he was 27 years old. At the beginning, we had much trouble. He did not hold his head properly, his arms flew all over, his balance was bad . . . But the dedication, the will-power of this man—there is none like him I have ever seen."

The amount of work that lay behind Bikila's magnificent achievements can be seen in this description of his training over an 11-day period in the summer of '60, before he left for Rome. (The training was done at an altitude of 5900 feet, about 25 miles from Addis Ababa.)

June 27—(Morning) 1 hour of varying work over the hills: 300 meters of climbing followed by 300 meters easy running to recuperate and so on. (Afternoon) 4 x 1500 meters on the track in times varying between 4:12 and 4:18 at five-minute intervals, then a sauna (Niskanen's influence; he's a Swede). Each training session was preceded and followed by 20 minutes of easy running to acclimatize Bikila's body both before and after exertion.

June 28—32 kilometers (nearly 20 miles) on road (without shoes) in 1:45.

June 29—Rest.

June 30—32 kilometers on road (with shoes) in 1:46:30.

July 1—(Morning) 5 x 1500 meters on the track at five-minute intervals, successively in 4:12, 4:18, 4:13, 4:14 and 4:14. (Afternoon) 45 minutes of running on varied ground.

July 2—Series of fast, straight runs on the track, interspersed with jogs around the turns. Duration: 45 minutes.

July 3—Rest.

July 4—(Morning) 1½ hours running on varied ground. (Afternoon) 3 x 1500 meters in 4:13, 4:15 and 4:15.

July 5—(Morning) 1 hour, 15 minutes of running on varied ground. (Afternoon) Easy run on gentle slopes, then a sauna.

July 6—Light training.

July 7—5000 meters on the track in 14:47.8 (actual time specified by Niskanen, 14:50).

And so it went. On July 26, 1960, as Bikila's training entered its final phase, he ran a marathon in 2:21:23. On Aug. 4, shortly before leaving for Rome, he ran 32 kilometers in 1:42:36 and Niskanen felt he could have continued at the same pace for the full marathon distance, which meant he would have finished in a time roughly equal to the world record at the time—2:15:17.

THE KENYANS REINFORCED THE IMAGE

The marvelous runners of Kenya, starting with the great Kip Keino in the mid-'60s, only reinforced the superman image begun by Bikila. The Kenyans did it as much by their numbers and their often unbelievably sudden emergence as by their performances. Remember Naftali Temu's victory over Ron Clarke in the 1966 Commonwealth Games six-mile? At the time, it boggled the mind. How, one wondered, was it possible for a runner no one had ever heard of before to beat a superstar such as Clarke—and in such a fast time (27:14.6, after a first three miles of 13:24.4). Of course, few, if any, of us realized that the little giant-killer Temu had competed in the Tokyo Olympics (although without distinction) two years earlier, and the next year had finished second to Keino and ahead of the highly-regarded Mamo Wolde in the 5000 meters at the East African Championships.

The Kenyan runners are obviously naturally talented, whatever the explanation for that talent might be, but talent alone, by the earlier definition, does not get them to the top anymore than it does a runner from any other country. As mentioned earlier in this book (see page 55), years of build-up are behind the peak performances of athletes like Keino and Jipcho. The remarkable Jipcho, currently Kenya's, and perhaps the world's, greatest distance runner, is probably the best example of individual human effort in Kenyan track. Although considered less naturally gifted than Keino, Jipcho has, by virtue of conscientious training, surpassed almost all of Keino's records and molded himself into a true superstar.

Evidence of Jipcho's hard training can even be seen in the way he has transformed himself physically. In 1968, when he first came to the attention of the track world by pacing Keino through the early stages of the 1500 in Mexico City, he looked heavy, almost muscle-bound. In 1973, when he put together a season perhaps unrivalled in distance running history and was voted track and field athlete of the year, he looked trim, hollow-cheeked, trained-down. That year he went undefeated in the steeplechase, first tying the world record (8:20.8), then lowering it twice—to 8:19.8 and then to 8:14.0. He ran a 3:52.0 mile, which only Jim Ryun had bettered, and an 8:16.4 two-mile, second fastest ever. He had several sensational doubles—like a 3:36.6 1500 the day after his 8:14.0 steeplechase, and an 8:18.2 steeplechase the day after his 3:52.0 mile. In Oslo on July 24 of that year he ran a 3:37.0 1500 and a 13:34.6 5000 within an hour!

Mel Watman described Jipcho's training in *Athletics Weekly* early in '74: "His training may, by British standards, seem light, but it must be remembered that all his training is carried out at high altitude. In 1971, he ran eight miles a day (Friday is a rest day). In May 1973, he decided to push his mileage up to 10 per day. Most of this is run on paths made of hard-packed cinders, and he reckons he operates at about five-minute miling pace ('I'm not very good at judging pace,' he admits with that infectious smile of his). For steeplechase workouts, he uses some crude homemade hurdles, between 3'2" and 3'6"—in order to make training that much harder." (The hurdles in the steeplechase are three feet high.)

Since early 1974, of course, Ben Jipcho has been with the International Track Association. As a professional, he has made it a habit of running and winning two distance races per night—usually with less than an hour's rest between. After his most impressive double as a professional (in Los Angeles, March 22, 1975, when he ran 8:27.0 for the two-mile and 3:56.2 for the mile with only 45 minutes rest in between), Jipcho gave this rather colorful description of his training: "I don't run very far. But I make it hard, make it painful. I bang on it. That makes it painful."

FULL CYCLE WITH AKII-BUA

In 1972 at Munich, 12 years after Abebe Bikila started the African running revolution, Uganda's John Akii-Bua brought it full cycle, winning the 400-meter hurdles in brilliant fashion to give Africa its first Olympic gold medal in a technique event. Running out of lane one—the slowest lane in the 400-meter hurdles—he won by a good five yards, clocking 47.8 to obliterate Dave Hemery's sensational world record of 48.1 set in Mexico City. *Athletics Weekly* called it "probably the greatest single track achievement of all time."

The most impressive thing about Akii-Bua's performance was the manner in which he held his hurdling form down the stretch. The 400-meter hurdles is an extremely punishing race. As Glenn Davis, the only man to win two Olympic gold medals in the event ('56 and '60) once explained to me, "When you run the 440-yard dash on the flat, you tend to tie up at the end, it's hard to move your legs. But in the 400-meter hurdles you've got to go over 10 hurdles as well. You're leaving the ground seven feet away from a hurdle and coming down four feet on the other side of the hurdle, and you're doing this all the way around the track. So your body has a tendency to get tight, to get heavy and towards the end of the race it's a strain to get over the hurdle. It's hard to get your lead leg up to clear the barrier and stay in proper hurdling form."

But at Munich John Akii-Bua looked as fast, loose and relaxed over the last two hurdles as he did over the first two. And after finishing, he amazingly had the energy left to jog happily around the track, waving his arms, throwing kisses to the crowd and jumping over hurdles (some real, some imaginary) as he went. Such as display, after so fast a run in so demanding a race, was all but unbelievable. In a way, it was reminiscent of Bikila's calisthenics in Tokyo.

After watching Akii-Bua's amazing performance in Munich, one was fully justified in asking: what is his secret, that he neither tires nor "ties up" like other men? I posed that question in a letter to Malcolm Arnold, who coached Akii-Bua for the four years prior to his Munich victory. Arnold, who was Uganda's national coach from '68 to '74 and is now the Welsh national coach, wrote back: "John Akii-Bua is a great athlete of his time because he was born wth the necessary attributes. He is intelligent, physically talented and, most important of all, very hard working. He worked at a very high level and his dedication was unquestionable. Usually he trained twice a day six days a week in conditions which were not ideal. All the tracks in Uganda were grass, which could get very wet in the period March-June every year. There were no weight training facilities which meant that any progressive resistance exercises had to be done in a makeshift way.

"I saw his victory in Munich as nothing more than a reward for his tremendously hard work over the preparation period and the manifestation of his talent. In the north of England, where I come from, they say 'You don't get owt for nowt,' which roughly translated means that you don't get something for nothing. John won his medal because he worked for it."

The severity of the training program John Akii-Bua undertook before Munich is probably without parallel in the history of the 400-meter hurdles. Philip Ndoo wrote a story on Akii-Bua for *The Daily Nation* after visiting him in Kampala in early 1972. Ndoo told me, "He was training a lot harder than some distance runners. He had been jogging up to 16 miles a day, although he had cut back to eight miles (a day) by the time I visited him."

This distance work was done during the first phase of Akii-Bua's training for Munich—"the build-up period", as Malcolm Arnold calls it. During the next stage of his training, the speed endurance period, typical workouts were: (a) 20 x 100 meters; (b) 20 x 150 meters; (c) 9 x 300 meters; (d) 6 x 600 meters or 800 meters, and (e) 4 x 1200 meters. Initially, the runs would be relatively slow and the rest between each run would be long. At the conclusion of this phase, the runs would be as fast as possible and the rest between each run would be short. At least 50% of this work was done over hurdles, and the 4 x 1200 meters was done with four or six hurdles per lap at 3'3", while wearing a weighted (25-pound) vest! (Akii-Bua told US runner-writer Kenny Moore that during the build-up phase of his training, he wore this same weighted vest in running six times up a 500-meter hill, twice a day!)

A speed phase completed Akii-Bua's preparation for Munich. During this period, he did runs at maximum speed with complete recovery between efforts. Again, the runs were done with and without hurdles. Malcolm Arnold wrote, "This phase of training lasted only the last 2-3 weeks before Munich, during which time he ran 46.18 seconds for 400 meters and the equivalent of 48.6 and 49.0 for the 400-meter hurdles, with only a 20-minute rest between the latter two runs."

Concluding his letter on Akii-Bua, Arnold said, "John's competitive spirit

Uganda's brilliant John Akii-Bua ... "One was fully justified in asking: what is his secret, that he neither tires nor 'ties up' like other men." (Tony Duffy)

was 101%, and best or nothing is usually the African attitude in this class of athlete. If they run well they remember, if they run badly the run is very soon forgotten. In all cases of African track success, please don't fall into the trap of crediting their performances to something mystical or strangely African. They achieve their success through hard work and nothing else. If you put their success down to other reasons you will be insulting them! They are no more and no less talented than any young person in Britain or America."

There are some people no doubt who will feel that Malcolm Arnold is being too conservative in his assessment of the African talent for running. Be that as it may, it should be abundantly clear by now that success has not been handed the African champions on the proverbial silver platter; they have had to reach for it, to work for it like other athletes around the world, and they should be respected for the effort behind their success as well as for the success itself.

MOHAMED GAMMOUDI

"A Runner Must Obey Himself"
by Pam Hadjeri

When one lists the greats of African distance running, Mohamed Gammoudi must rank at or near the very top. Although the quiet, modest Tunisian has never received the worldwide attention in the press that such other African runners as Kip Keino, Ben Jipcho and Filbert Bayi have, there isn't a runner anywhere who's had a more impressive and consistent Olympic record over the last 15 years. He is, for example, the only runner to have won a medal in each of the last three Olympic Games. And, as Pam Hadjeri reports here, Gammoudi's Olympic string may not be over.

Pam Hadjeri is American, her husband Tunisian, and they live in southern California. This article was written in the fall of '74 after Pam had interviewed Gammoudi on a visit to Tunisia with her husband. "He spoke mostly Arabic," she says of Gammoudi, "which was translated by my husband to French, which I jotted down in English."

If that sounds complicated, it was nothing compared to the difficulty of actually setting up the interview. Says Pam, "It was an adventure getting to him: we had to pass through the police, the Army, Air Tunis, a cousin and some friends. We tried to meet him four different times in four different places before we finally reached him at home, where he received us royally. At one point we had been mysteriously sitting in a sidewalk cafe in downtown Tunis waiting for an unknown person to pick us up. The person was 1½ hours late."

Mohamed Gammoudi, with four Olympic medals from the Tokyo, Mexico City and Munich Games, ought to be enjoying his retirement. And, in fact, he has practically disappeared from competition since the '72 Olympics when a fall knocked him out of the 10,000 meters, but he came back to win the silver medal in the 5000. Gammoudi, however, continues to train regularly. At 36, after 14 years of top-class racing, he hopes for still another Olympic medal—this time in the marathon.

Despite his Olympic and international successes, Gammoudi is relatively unknown and thus something of an enigma. He comes from Tunisia, a small North African country with strong French ties but relatively unknown to the West, in sports at least. Language has always been a barrier in interviewing Gammoudi, who speaks Arabic and a little French. However, it is sports history that this soldier from North Africa has taken the track world by surprise more than once. Since 1962, his famous kick has helped him win major international victories over Ron Clarke, Kip Keino, Michel Jazy and others. His longevity as a champion is exceptional. Just when everyone thinks that Gammoudi's career is finished (as after the Mexico Olympics where he won a gold medal in the 5000 and a bronze in the 10,000 meters), he again takes his place at the starting line, as in Munich, produces his best times and wins another medal.

The Tunisian Army was the first to be surprised in 1959 when Gammoudi, a shy recruit, began to break records. He ran his first race for high stakes: a leave from boot camp. Anxious and homesick for the rough, desert terrain of Sidi Aich in south central Tunisia where he was born, Gammoudi placed third. Sidi Aich was the birthplace of prehistoric Caspian man, who left flints and shells centuries before the Romans arrived. The land offers little distraction or relief, and children run all day, pushing a hoop round and round with a stick. It is rumored that people hunt jackrabbits by running in relays, chasing them until the animals drop from exhaustion. Running is important to survival in this arid and ancient part of the world.

If running was natural to Gammoudi, so was winning. In 1960, he entered a nationwide, military cross-country race in his hometown. He placed first and was immediately sent to Orvetto, Italy, for three months of intensive training. He returned home and broke the Tunisian 5000-meter record by nine seconds, running 14:54. A year later, he brought the record down to 14:41 and was assigned to the Center for Military Sports, where he would train for serious competiton.

Until 1962, Gammoudi was known only to the Tunisian Army. He had run respectable times, but international competition was far removed from boot camp races. He first created a stir outside Tunis at the CISM (International Council for Military Sports) Games in Amsterdam in 1962. He was unknown and without a speciality. His trainers wondered where to enter him. His best 1500 time of 3:52.8 seemed slow, so Gammoudi was entered in the 10,000 meters against the seven-time champion, Henri Clerckx of Belgium. In a startling upset, Gammoudi placed first with 29:50. Shaken, Clerckx vowed to beat the unknown Tunisian in the 5000 meters and openly presented a challenge. But in the race Gammoudi quietly took the lead at the 3000-meter mark and held it until the Belgian gave up. Gammoudi won again, in 14:18.8.

These were the first of many gold medals. In 1963, he returned home with victories in the 5000 meters at both the Jeux Mediterraneens in Naples and the Jeux de l'Amitee in Dakar. French sportswriters began to take notice of the Tunisian soldier who presented a real threat to such French stars as Michel Jazy and Michel Bernard. L'Equipe predicted that Gammoudi might be a surprise in the 1964 Tokyo Olympics.

However, none of his competitors were worried about him when he arrived in Tokyo with a relatively poor qualifying time of 29:36 for the 10,000 meters. It was thus a shock to see the slender, dark-haired Tunisian among the leading group of four—with favorite Ron Clarke and two other surprises, American Billy Mills

(Top) Mexico City, 1968—Mohamed Gammoudi fights off Kip Keino to win the 5000, with Naftali Temu third. (Bottom) Happy winner flanked by the two somber Kenyans. (Top photo, Ed Lacey; bottom photo, Mark Shearman)

and Ethiopia's Mamo Wolde—as the race entered the final eight laps. Wolde dropped off with 2½ laps to go (apparently having injured a calf muscle), and going into the bell lap of that historic race it was Clarke leading, with Mills on his shoulder and Gammoudi right behind.

About halfway through the first bend Clarke found himself in danger of being hemmed in by Mills behind a lapped runner (a barefooted African who only four years later would win the Olympic gold medal in this event—Naftali Temu). In his book *The Unforgiving Minute*, Clarke explained what happened next:

"I started to shove into the American's shoulder and he leaned back into me. There seemed only one thing to do. I crashed Billy with my right arm, and whether he exaggerated the effect I don't know, but he careened three or four lanes across the track, then veered in again. As he did so, I stepped around the lapped runner while Mohamed, seeing an opening, burst through the opening created by my whack.

"The Tunisian was only half-way through when Billy narrowed the gap. Mohamed put one hand on each of us and wedged his way through and ran hard. Off balance myself, I let Mohamed open a couple of yards' lead before trying to catch him. Billy disappeared from view."

The dash for the tape was on. Gammoudi led, Clarke chasing hard, all the way around into the homestretch—the two of them threading their way through lapped runners (a massive field of 40 had started the race). Clarke would later compare that last lap to a "dash for a train in a peak-hour crowd." Coming down the homestretch Clarke drew even but Gammoudi surprised the Australian by forcing himself a foot or two ahead. Suddenly Billy Mills flew by both of them at an unbelievable speed down the outside to score one of the great upsets in Olympic history. Gammoudi was second, in 28:24.8, only four-tenths of a second behind Mills. Both of them broke the existing Olympic record.

Gammoudi returned from the Tokyo Games to an ecstatic homeland, which received its first international athletic hero with much fanfare. Tunisia is a Muslim country where humility is a virtue, will-power an expression of faith, and Olympic gold medal winners one in five million. More than 10 years after Tokyo, Gammoudi is still an adored hero to his countrymen.

It was the month of Ramadan, when Muslims fast from dawn to dusk to show their humility and will-power as an act of faith, that Gammoudi met with us. Even water is forbidden until sunset, and Gammoudi admitted he was tired from fasting, expecially as he trained twice a day in the hot, autumn sun. It was night, and he sipped Turkish coffee scented with orange blossoms and ate traditional pudding extracted from filberts.

Gammoudi claims to follow no special diet except to keep his weight low. He has never heard of ERG athletic drink or the carbohydrate-loading diet. A Muslim, he neither smokes nor drinks. He tries to eat what is natural, by which he means simple food: protein, fruits and vegetables. The Tunisians, proud of Gammoudi and their cuisine, laughingly claim he eats couscous before a race. (For the uninitiated, couscous is a North African speciality of semoule, meat and vegetables and lays like cement on even the most hardy stomachs.) A recent Tunisian biography on Gammoudi boasts that his daily diet includes five yogurts, 10 fruits, four teas, two coffees, two pastries, an enormous amount of meat, fish, cheese and milk, and as much parsley as he desires.

Gammoudi's talent and consistency, however, are not easily ascribed to any one thing. His performances between the Tokyo and Mexico Olympics continued to establish his name. The Tokyo success was followed by a 27:38.2 victory in the six miles at the 1965 British Championships in London. He returned in 1966 and defended his title against British star Dick Taylor by sprinting from 800 meters out, a change from his usual 400-meter kick. A furious battle ensued to the 200-meter mark before Taylor finally gave up. Gammoudi was clocked in 27:14.6.

Then the troubles began. Like many runners, Gammoudi has had his share of aches and pains. He showed us his big toes—grey and crenelated—and laughed. His serious trouble, in a career relatively free of injury, started in 1966 with recurring achilles tendon problems. In 1966, glands in his throat were removed. A Swiss doctor and sportsman, Dr. Jean-Paul Martin, claimed they were responsible for his tendon problems. Three months later, Gammoudi was training for Mexico City, trouble-free.

By the 1968 Olympic Games, Gammoudi calculates he had run a distance equal to twice around the Equator. Preparing for Mexico City, he had averaged 800 kilometers a month and had promised his countrymen a medal. A man of his word, but modest, Gammoudi did even better: a gold medal for the 5000 meters, in a superb tactical race in which he held off Kip Keino over the last lap (to the amazement of many) and a bronze medal for the 10,000. These performances were especially impressive considering that, contrary to popular belief, he was not a high-altitude native like the Kenyans and Ethiopeans. He had spent considerable time training at altitude in France before the Games, but no more than other "lowland" runners. (*Editor:* According to Ron Clarke, the secret of Gammoudi's success at Mexico City is that, unlike other top sea-level runners, he raced as often as possible at altitude in the two years prior to the Games and his altitude training was specifically geared to finding out his capabilities and limitations at altitude. One altitude workout Clarke saw Gammoudi doing was 3-4 x 3000 meters—first 1000 easy, second 1000 at about 5000-meter pace and last 1000 as fast as possible. When Clarke tried the workout at sea level, he found it extremely difficult! Says Clarke of Gammoudi: "He knew exactly his limitations at altitude. . . No one prepared better for the Games in Mexico than Mohammed.")

After Mexico City, Gammoudi announced he would like to try again for an Olympic medal. But his hopes were brighter than his performances for the next four years. He ran some respectable races (a silver medal in the Jeux Mediterraneens, 1971, 5000 meters in 13:40.8), but his performances were inconsistent, even in cross-country, which has always been his forte. When Gammoudi dropped out of the CISM world championsip cross-country race in February of 1972, track experts generally assumed it was the end of his long and exciting career. However, Gammoudi was too busy training for Munich to read reviews.

He arrived in Munich for his third Olympic Games, a fresh, strong, ambitious athlete. He qualified for the 10,000-meter final with his best time ever: 27:54.8. Then disaster! About midway through the final Lasse Viren fell in front of him and Gammoudi went tumbling over the Finn onto the infield. Viren was able to rise quickly and rejoin the pack. But Gammoudi remained stunned on the infield for several seconds. When he finally arose to take up the chase, the lead runners were far down the track. He continued for 600 meters, saw his task was futile and then stopped. Gammoudi's hopes were crushed; he admitted he had trained for 10,00 meters and didn't feel as fit for the 5000. Nonetheless, he ran a superb 5000, clocking 13:27.4, to win his second silver and fourth Olympic medal.

After twelve years of racing and four Olympic medals, Gammoudi decided to withdraw from competition. He had run a good last race; as Captain, his military career was assured; he had served his country well. He was married and building a lovely white rock and stucco home facing the Bardo Museum in Tunis. He wanted time for his home, his farm, his family. At 34, Gammoudi retired.

But not for long. In March 1974, the Tunisian Army needed a representative to enter the 10,000-meter CISM Military Cross-Country Championships in Morocco. Gammoudi was still the best choice. He had retired from competition but had never stopped running. He very reluctantly agreed to enter, afraid he would only be an embarrassing reminder of his better days. Gammoudi surprised himself this time. Without serious training, he placed fourth against well-trained and younger runners.

Since May 1974, Gammoudi has increased his training. As in the past, he is his own pupil and coach. In the 14 years of his career, Gammoudi has only had a coach for four of those years—a Czechoslovakian coached him for three years, and a Tunisian for one year. Even as a member of the Center of Military Sports, with all its facilities and coaches, Gammoudi has obeyed his own intuition in training. He has attended short clinics abroad for one to three months training, usually before a big race. He has no set training pattern, but runs interval sessions two or three times a week (e.g., perhaps as many as 20 x 400 meters—in sets of four or five—in 52-56 seconds with a 400-meter jog). On other days, he takes long runs, up to 25 kilometers. He never runs alone. Recently, Gammoudi spent a month training in Fontainebleu, France, and has run a few 5000-meter races in Paris with an impressive best time of 13:39.

But now Gammoudi is interested in hours, not minutes, and kilometers, not meters. He wants to run and win a medal in the marathon at the 1976 Montreal Olympics. It is hardly a modest proposal from an otherwise shy man. Gammoudi admits the difficulty. He has never run the marathon distance, but recently competed in a 25-kilometer road race in Italy and ran 1:16. In his 25-kilometer training runs, he finishes a good kilometer ahead of his training companions, but that is the greatest distance he has attempted. He intends to gradually increase his distance, but will try only one or two marathon runs before Montreal.

Gammoudi insists that his training is and must be natural, free of extreme diets and schedules which cannot be maintained over a long time. He feels that excessive training methods doom many athletes, especially the Americans, to short-lived careers. The man bears listening to, considering that his best times for the 3000, 5000 and 10,000 meters were all run in 1972, eight years after his auspicious Olympic debut in Tokyo!

Gammoudi very simply explains that his remarkable longevity as a champion is due to dedication, ambition and moderation. He admits he was gifted and versatile. In addition to his achievements in the 5000 and 10,000 meters, he has run the 800 in 1:50.1, the 1000 in 2:23.3 and the 1500 in 3:41.9. He repeats that he always wanted to win, and like all runners he needed courage. In Gammoudi's words, "A runner must obey himself."

He talks about winning again: he will try the marathon at the Jeux Mediterraneens in Algeria and possibly at the US vs. Africa meet in 1975. The Montreal Olympics will then be only one year away. Gammoudi smiles, and one gets the feeling that here is a man who knows how to obey himself.

MAMO WOLDE

Out of the Shadow of Bikila

by Geoff Fenwick

**Another African distance runner who's had an unusually long and success-
ful career is Ethiopia's Mamo Wolde. Now retired, Wolde first competed in the
Olympics in 1956, the first year his country entered the Games. He won the last
of his three Olympic medals 16 years later in Munich at age 40! Here Geoff Fenwick, who knows Mamo Wolde and followed his career over the years, writes
about this little Ethiopian who used to run in the giant shadow of Abebe Bikila
but emerged from it to cast quite a shadow of his own.**

Slim, diminutive, at about 5'7", 117 lbs., and with the cadaverous cheeks
of a hard-training long distance runner, Mamo Wolde was just about the last athlete one would expect to have a lengthy career. Yet this little man competed at
the highest level for 16 years starting with the Melbourne Olympics in 1956 and
ending with the 1972 Olympics, where he won a bronze medal in the marathon.
Between those dates he had competed in four Olympic Games and had placed
first, second, third and fourth in his best four Olympic races. I can think of no
other long distance runner of modern times who was so successful for so long.

It was never a case of roses all the way for Mamo though; success did not
come easily. His Olympic debut was inauspicious enough, for in Melbourne in
1956 he finished last in his heat of the 1500 meters, and ran the third leg of
Ethiopia's 4 x 400 relay team which also finished last in its heat. One would expect such results in 1956. Wolde was young and inexperienced, and besides, African runners merely "made up the numbers" in those days.

The Melbourne trip was followed by a lengthly period of obscurity for him.
Ethiopia has never been an easy place from which to obtain information and
whether Wolde retired or merely concentrated on domestic competition is not
known. He did not go to the Rome Olympics in 1960. His countrymen and
fellow soldier Abebe Bikila did, however, and his marathon victory there is now
history.

Bikila's victory was an inspiration to a whole continent's athletes and no
doubt it gave Wolde renewed motivation. Both he and Bikila were members of
the Emperor of Ethiopia's bodyguard and they trained together over the stony
terrain surrounding the capital city of Addis Ababa. After 1960 Bikila was much
in demand internationally and when he went abroad to compete, Wolde went,
too.

Between 1962 and 1966, Wolde was extremely active. He travelled exten-
sively, competing in Asia, Europe, Africa and North America. Notable among
his victories was his success in an international cross-country event in Spain in
the hard winter of 1972. When I spoke with him some months later, he recalled
with some amusement how he had reacted to the unaccustomed cold. He had
not felt it too much during the race but when he smiled as he crossed the finish

line, his countenance literally froze and for two hilarious minutes he wandered around looking like a ventriloquist's dummy. During the next year he was to repeat his Spanish victory and win a track race over 15 miles in world record time in the United States.

During these years, Wolde trained hard, covering between five and 18 miles daily in training, often in the heat of the day. Gradually he established himself as one of the most formidable 10,000-meter runners in Africa. This distance was the one he liked best. He could remember Kuts and Pirie from the Melbourne Olympics and his wish was to be as good as those world famous runners had been. It was obvious he was coming close to achieving his aim. At high altitude he was unbeatable. Between 1962 and 1964 he won 10,000-meter races in Cairo, Kampala and Nairobi, beating the best East Africans, including Anentia and the young Temu, with ease. In Nairobi he encountered European and American runners and demolished them. In Kampala he almost lapped the field, winning a six-mile race in 28:30.4 at an altitude of 4000 feet and on a warm day.

Shortly before the Tokyo Olympics in 1964, I wrote of him: "In high altitude, tropical countries, it's doubtful if anyone can beat this Ethiopian. In the Olympics, of course, it will be different but don't be surprised if Mamo Wolde is up with the leaders in Tokyo." This proved to be a reasonable forecast, for Mamo finished fourth in Tokyo, being dropped only in the last three laps.

Although this result was highly commendable, Wolde seemed to be discouraged at the time. He was still in the shadow of Bikila, for that remarkable runner had registered his second consecutive Olympic marathon victory. In the years after Tokyo, Wolde seemed to have lost the will to succeed. He was in his mid-30s and his track career seemed to be coming to an end. In the African Games at Brazzaville in 1965 he finished a dispirited third in the 5000 meters behind Keino and Temu. There were signs of recovery in the cross-country season of 1967-68, however, and he returned to Spain for a third time to win, yet again, an international cross-country race.

Obviously, experience at altitude would be a decisive factor at the Olympic Games in Mexico City in 1968. Yet Wolde did not seem to have recaptured his form of earlier years and for all his advantage of high-altitude existence he was not one of the favorites in the 10,000 meters. Not for the first time, he defied expectations and won his first Olympic medal, a silver, after a stirring last lap battle in which he led Naftali Temu from the bell into the homestraight only to be passed by the Kenyan in the last 50 meters. Only three meters separated them at the finish. Mohamed Gammoudi was third and for the first time in history Africans occupied all three steps of the Olympic victory stand.

After that fine performance by Wolde, at age 36, it was easy to assume that the track world had seen the culmination of his Olympic career. Few thought he had any chance in the marathon. Bikila was there yet again (and hadn't Bikila once said, "Mamo can compete with me but I know I will beat Mamo"?) Plus Wolde's marathon record was distinctly suspect. On several occasions (including Boston in 1963), he had gone out too fast in the early stages and had faded badly (although at Boston, the cold may have been the cause). In the marathon at Tokyo in '64 he had dropped out, apparently due to injury.

Yet once more Mamo proved his critics wrong, scoring a decisive victory while Bikila failed to finish. Wolde started the race conservatively. At five kilometers, with Bikila up with the leaders, Mamo bided his time 20 seconds off the

Mamo Wolde waves to the crowd after winning the marathon at Mexico City in '68. His victory gave Ethiopia its third consecutive Olympic gold medal in the event. (Mark Shearman)

pace. By 10 kilometers Bikila had disappeared from the front rank due to an injury and Wolde had closed to within three seconds of the lead. Bikila would finally drop out after 17 kilometers because of the injury, which doctors diagnosed as a fracture of the fibula bone in his left leg. Afterwards, Bikila explained through interpreters: "If this had been my first Olympics, I would have made an effort to go on. But I have already won two championships, and the pain was so great I felt I just couldn't continue. Besides, Mamo was ahead and I felt he could win the race."

Bikila's confidence in his countryman wasn't misplaced. By 20 kilometers only four runners were left at the front—Europeans Gaston Roelants and Tim Johnston, followed closely by Wolde and Naftali Temu. By 25 kilometers the two Africans had broken away, Temu now leading Wolde by eight seconds, with the next runner almost half a minute behind. Wolde overtook Temu in the next five kilometers, and while the Kenyan faded badly after that (eventually finishing 19th), Wolde ran on steadily to win by the overwhelming margin of more than three minutes. Looking as fresh at the finish as Bikila did in Tokyo, Wolde jogged more than a full lap on the grass outside the track, smiling and blowing kisses to the cheering crowd, before the next runner appeared. Mamo Wolde had taken over Abebe Bikila's crown and given Ethiopia its third consecutive gold medal in the Olympic marathon. His winning time was 2:20.26.

Mamo's victory was a popular one, for his quiet modesty had gained him many friends among his fellow athletes. It would not be realistic to claim that the altitude at Mexico played no part in his success. But it was a fine win nonetheless. For one thing, it would be difficult to imagine a more perfectly-paced race—at altitude or anywhere else. The difference between Mamo's time for the first 20 kilometers of the race and the second 20 kilometers was *one second!*— 1:06:28 to 1:06:29.

Following Mexico one might have been excused for thinking that Mamo Wolde's Olympic career was now at an end. During the next four years he competed only rarely outside Ethiopia. He was not strikingly successful in the marathon races he ran in Europe and Asia, although he was never badly beaten either. When the first United States-Africa track meet was held in the US in 1971, Wolde wasn't on the African team. One of the Ethiopian runners on the team, the then-unknown Miruts Yifter, explained through an interpreter: "Wolde is just preparing for the marathon now." It was clear that little Mamo Wolde was far too proud to relinquish his Olympic title by default. And so he returned to the Olympic Games for the fourth time in 16 years.

No one gave him much chance now. The Munich Olympics were not at 7400 feet above sea level like the Mexico City Olympics and thus Mamo's greatest advantage had been lost. Plus there were many runners in the race who had much more impressive records in the two years before Munich than Mamo did— athletes like Ron Hill, Frank Shorter, Karel Lismont, Lutz Philipp, and others. Yet Mamo produced what might be considered his finest race, finishing third in world-class time, 2:15:08, running against many athletes who were fresh out of kindergarten when he competed in the Olympics for the first time. For Mamo was now 40 years old!

Now in retirement at last, Mamo Wolde lives in a country where society has suddenly erupted into mass turbulence. Emperor Haile Selassie, the man whom Mamo Wolde and Abebe Bikila served as members of the Imperial Bodyguard, was deposed in the summer of '74. Late in '74 the world read reports of fighting between Ethiopia's national forces and secessionists in the northern Ethiopian city of Asmara. But as I look at the red, green and gold Imperial badge Mamo Wolde gave me so long ago, I am certain that whatever the changes and turbulence in his country, the modest but supremely determined Mamo will weather the storm.

NAFTALI TEMU

The Forgotten Champion
by Philip Ndoo

Kenya's Naftali Temu scored one of the great upsets in track history when he beat Australia's Ron Clarke in the six mile at the '66 British Commonwealth Games. Two years later the 5'7½", 130-pound Kisii runner became Kenya's first Olympic gold medallist when he won the 10,000, as well as placing third in the 5,000, at the Mexico City Olympics. Due to the altitude factor, however, he was never given full credit for his Olympic victory. Philio Ndoo, who was a teammate of Temu's on the 1970 Commonwealth Games team, writes about this great little runner who was forced into premature retirement by injury and is now a forgotten champion—even in his own country.

"...I have won the gold in the Commonwealth Games, I have won gold in the Olympics, now all I want is to set a world record." That was Naftali Temu speaking of his goal and ambition one year before the 1972 Olympics.

Temu, a modest and likeable individual, was talking casually, but deep inside he was expressing bitterness. I had gone to the Nairobi Airport to meet a team of five Kenyans who were returning from a European tour which included competition in the pre-Olympics held in Munich, September 1971.

Since his success at the 1968 Mexico Olympics, where he won the gold medal in the 10,000 meters, Temu had gone through a period of frustration. His success at the Mexico Olympics had been attributed to advantage at altitude. He knew he was capable of matching the best in the world at his distance, but for some reason he had not been given his due credit and respect. At home, of course, the Kisii soldier had to contend with second spot, prestige-wise, behind the legendary Kipchoge Keino.

"Now tell me, I beat that Clarke they were talking about in Jamaica, and tell me... were there mountains in Kingston?" Temu said.

The cause for frustration on this particular day was the fact that Temu's performance on the tour had been overlooked. And rightly so, since the then-rising Ben Jipcho was performing hitherto unheard of wonders, winning the steeplechase in the pre-Munich Games after two nasty falls, following that up with victory the second day in the 5000 meters against such stars as Ian Stewart and Lasse Viren, and a week later winning the mile in a classy field which included, among others, Keino, Jurgen May and Francesco Arese. No wonder Temu's career best of 13:36.4 for 5000 meters during that tour went unnoticed!

Since the Mexico Olympics, Temu's training had been hampered by an achilles tendon injury, which he'd received in July of 1969 while running in an international meet in Italy. In that meet, Temu had lost to the then miler-briefly-turned 10,000-meter runner Francesco Arese. The Italians went wild when Arese, in his first trial at this distance, downed the Olympic champion.

As it turned out, that injury eventually was to force Temu into a premature retirement, by African standards, at age 28.

A year before the Mexico City Olympics in 1968, Naftali Temu was a convincing winner of the 10,000 meters in the US-Commonwealth meet in Los Angeles. He became Kenya's first Olympic gold medallist when he won the 10,000 on the opening day of the '68 Olympics. (Jeff Kroot)

After 1969, Temu had struggled to prove that his success in Mexico City was no fluke but to no avail. He made a brief comeback in 1970, qualifying for the Commonwealth Games held in Edinburgh, Scotland. As the field went to the starting line, it seemed as though Ron Clarke, never a winner in major Games competition, had been given a third chance against the Kenyan, but midway through the race, this anticipated showdown faded. Temu slowed down, and was obviously in great pain from his injury. As I went past him with half a mile to go, lapping him for the first time in my running career, he shouted, *"Fuata, kibisha mwananchi"* (Swahili for "Follow, go get them, buddy"). In his tone was a note of despair. His encouragement helped a bit, though. I overtook three people to take seventh. But if the two of us were disappointed, Clarke was also. This was his last chance to win a gold medal, and he lost it, being outsprinted in the homestraight by the relatively unknown Lachie Stewart.

Disappointed but not discouraged, Temu went back home and laid off for nearly six months for the injury to heal. After he resumed running, things seemed promising, at least as far as his health was concerned. But qualifying for Munich turned out to be a rather close call. After his poor performances the entire first half of the year, even the most fanatical Temu fans in Kenya had given up hopes of him making the Kenyan team. But in the Kenya trials held in Mombasa, Temu turned in probably his best performance ever to qualify for his third Olympics. Running on a loose sandy track, he upset the pre-race favorite Richard Juma, winning in a career best of 28:21.4 for the 10,000 meters (see page 54). The time still stands as the fastest on African soil.

A month before Munich, however, the injury developed again. The best he could do in the Games was to finish 12th in the first heat of the 10,000.

Like his Kenyan colleagues, Temu started running when he was in elementary school, and participated in local track meets in his teens, winning most of them. He lost some to his elder brother, who Temu believes would have developed into a better athlete than he. Naftali's first taste of major competition was the 1964 Tokyo Olympics, where he competed in the 10,000 meters (in bare feet) and the marathon, but he failed to place in both races.

His Tokyo experience paid off a year later when he competed in the first All-Africa Games held in Brazzaville, the Congo, where his 13:58.4 effort landed him a silver medal in the 5000 meters behind Keino's 13:44.4. The following year he received invitations to compete in several meets in Europe. His season culminated in August with the British Commonwealth Games in Kingston, Jamaica.

In Jamaica, Temu was still unknown, and among those who paid little attention to the small but big-chested Kenyan was multi-record holder and superstar of the Games, Ron Clarke, who later said, "I remember meeting him vaguely (in Europe)." (Temu had been fourth earlier that year in a 5000-meter race in Berlin won by Keino, with Clarke second.)

Prior to the six-mile, in which Clarke was the overwhelming favorite, Kenyan coach John Velzian says he spent considerable time with Temu persuading him that he could beat the Australian. Clarke set a tremendous pace from the gun (13:24.4 for the first three miles), but Temu stayed with him. When four laps remained Temu shot ahead and went on to win with a commanding lead. But the last lap turned into a bizarre and frightening experience for him.

Temu now relates that when he sprinted with one lap to go, he could see Clarke behind his shoulder. "I saw him pull ahead of me in the far stretch, but I pulled slightly ahead around the final bend, then he pulled ahead of me in the homestretch. There I just closed my eyes and ran as fast as I could, but I could not catch him. When I reached the finish line I thought he had beaten me..." Temu relates. Temu thought his colleagues were kidding him when they told him he had beaten Clarke by nearly 150 yards. It so happened that the meet was held at night and Temu was chasing his own shadow! He set a Games record of 27:14.6, running his last lap in 59 seconds.

In Mexico, the story was just as dramatic and memorable. For years, Temu had run in the shadow of Keino and although he had beaten him at least once, Sept. 23, 1967, in the three miles, and was more experienced in the longer 10,000 meters, Keino was still considered the favorite in Kenya to win the 10,000 at Mexico City. In the race Keino fell onto the grass due to a gall bladder attack three laps from the finish, but Temu didn't know this at the time. "When I looked back and saw that there was no Keino, and there was half a lap to go, I decided to give it all I had," he said. His finishing sprint, of course, gave him a narrow victory over Ethiopia's Mamo Wolde.

Africans mature late, and at the age of 28 in 1972, Temu still had several years of competition left. However, the talented, already-proven Olympic champion retired with one of his ambitions—that of setting a world record—unfulfilled. Temu is now the forgotten champion. The rise of Ben Jipcho in Kenya, after the lapse of Keino, did not help matters. Although Temu's performances could justifiably warrant him a place among the greats of the sport, to many his name is among the "one-race performers."

Temu is now an officer in charge of physical training at the Kenya Army Physical Training College, Lanet, near Nakuru. He is married, with three children.

KIPCHOGE KEINO

Kenya's Finest Ambassador
by Philip Ndoo

Kipchoge Keino's accomplishments on the track are familiar to running fans around the world. Yet one may wonder how many people really appreciate how great a runner the long-striding Kenyan has been. A point that's almost never made about him, for instance, is that he surely has to rate as the greatest all-round distance runner (and one is tempted to say natural runner) the world has yet seen. What other runner has produced the marks that Keino has over so wide a range of distances—from 1500 meters all the way up to 10,000 meters? (And don't forget the steeplechase.)

In view of Keino's remarkable versatility there's no telling how many world records he could have set had he been more "record oriented." For example, the world two-mile record should have been his for the asking, considering his mile-three mile capability (3:53.1, 12:57.4). But with the exception of a few

races, Keino chose to run against the man rather than against the clock. As he
once told this writer, "A man can't serve two masters. Ron Clarke serves two masters: he runs to set world records and he runs to win. I serve only one master: I
run to win."

Ironically, the greatest of the two world records that Keino did set—his
7:39.5 for 3000 meters, run in 1965—was never fully appreciated, particularly in
North America where people are not familiar with the distance. In fact, that
record was the equivalent of about an 8:15 two-mile and was a performance truly
ahead of its time. Today, a decade later, the world outdoor two-mile record is
still only 8:13.8, although the 3000 record has been lowered to 7:35.2 (to achieve
that time Brendan Foster of Great Britain averaged 60.7 seconds per lap for 7½ laps!)

Thousands of words have been written about Kip Keino, including a full-
length biography. In the following article Keino's friend and fellow runner,
Philip Ndoo, offers a unique personal look at the incomparable Kenyan.

Whenever people talk of East Africa or even the entire African continent,
one of the three names—Kenya, Kenyatta and Keino—must enter the conversation. Politicians cannot talk of Africa without mentioning the Kenyan President,
Keino's name is synonymous with sports in Africa, and Kenya is generally known
as the country which produces super-runners.

Since bursting into prominence in 1965, Hezekiah Kipchoge Keino, son of
Kipkeino arap Kurgat, has won numerous honors for his country and himself. In
Kenya, youngsters identify themselves with his name whenever they challenge each
other to a race. Two streets and as many stadiums have been named after him.
Above all, President Jomo Kenyatta has twice recognized the man who has risked
his life on the track, literally, for the sake of his country. The Kenyan head of
state has bestowed the Order of the Burning Spear and the Distinguished Con-
duct Medal on the "flying policeman" who once guarded him while the President
was a political detainee before the country's independence. But despite all these
honors and the glory, the son of a herdsman-peasant farmer remains humble and
his behavior is exemplary.

Keino's athletic achievements, which easily qualify him as one of the sport's
all-time greats, can be summed up in doubles. Two Olympic gold and silver medals, two Olympic records, once holder of two world records, winner of two gold
medals at the '66 Commonwealth Games and, possibly his greatest achievement,
a fantastic mile-three mile double of 3:53.1 and 13:31.6 on the same day (at
Kisumu, Kenya in 1967). Those times would probably have been faster on a better track and at a more favorable altitude. The Kisumu track, though one of the
fastest in East Africa, is sometimes bumpy and is located more than 4000 feet
above sea level.

As a youth, Keino experienced adversities reminiscent of characters in fic-
tion episodes. On several occasions, he missed death from fierce leopards and
poisonous snakes. At one time, he had to sleep in a tree for three nights to escape the wrath of a cruel uncle with whom he was then living. As a Nandi, Keino
had to go through the demanding circumcision rituals, a near torture experience
which by tradition is supposed to toughen the Nandi into fearless warriors— and
fearless this warrior is.

Keino was one of the pre-race favorites in three events—the 10,000, 5000 and
1500—in the Mexico Olympics, but a gall bladder ailment during the duration of

The man whose name is synonomous with African running—Kipchoge Keino. Through his many victories, the great Kenyan did more than any other man to put Kenya, and Africa, on the athletic map of the world. (Mark Shearman)

the Games handicapped his chances. In the 10,000 meters, for instance, he was with the leaders with three laps to go when he became dizzy and crashed to the ground in the infield, thus being eliminated. But even though he was told of the seriousness of the illness by a West German doctor, and despite the protestations of Kenyan team coach Charles Mukora, who is his personal friend and a business partner, Keino risked his health and "ran the 1500 meters for his country."

If that is not proof enough of Keino's courage (some people could speculate that his illness in Mexico City was "not serious"), there is the incident at the 1970 British Commonwealth Games in Edinburgh. I was sharing a room with Keino on the second floor of the Edinburgh University dorm. It was around four o'clock in the afternoon when he walked into the room. I could tell something was wrong because his seemingly perpetual smile was missing. With sunken eyes and a pale face, he said in Swahili, *"Wanataka kuhua mimi,"* ("They want to kill me.") I interpreted this to mean that he was upset perhaps because the officials wanted him to run in another event—like the 10,000 meters in addition to the 1500 and 5000 which he had entered already. Then he added that he had received an unsigned letter telling him that he would be shot if he competed in the 5000 meters.

I had been working as a sports reporter for the *Daily Nation* for two years by that time, and this would have been the scoop of my career. But Ben Gethi, the commandant of the Kenya contingent, commanded me not to say a word to the *Nation* or any of my press colleagues. Dutifully I complied and later came within an inch of losing my job, since the news leaked out and our competitor back in Kenya got it first.

But that week was one of the longest I have ever experienced. The worst part came just before the final of the 5000 meters. Keino had moved to another room by then, but I happened to be with him when he was warming up for the event. He looked even worse than the day he received the first threat. This time he had received a telephone call, warning him that he would be shot if he tried to win the race. I had no suggestions to offer but his words—"a man dies only once"—left me speechless. He ran the race and finished third behind Ian Stewart's Games record time of 13:22.8. Keino's time was 13:27.6, then his third fastest for the distance.

The worry of the competition itself is enough to exhaust many athletes, but for someone to go through the ordeal Keino did and still run such a time is remarkable indeed. Perhaps this helps answer the question of why the African athletes seem to worry less before competition than athletes from other countries. They worry, but maybe they are able to handle or overcome the worry better than their counterparts.

Keino has been labelled "Kenya's finest ambassador", and he fully deserves such an honor. But it is perhaps his diplomatic approach to problems, most of them from Kenya AAA officials, which qualifies him as a true diplomat. Unlike Ben Jipcho, or the outspoken Robert Ouko, Keino would go to great trouble, even sacrifice his time, to achieve a compromise and protect the KAAA officials from blame. Some say he did most of these things because, as a policeman, he had to obey orders, and could not criticize his superiors. But both Jipcho and Ouko are officers in the Prisons Department and are subject to the same discipline.

One time I met Keino at the Nairobi Airport on his return from a meet in Europe. He told me, "Do not write this in your paper, but I will never go out with that official again as my manager. He treated me like an animal. We were given a room with two beds but he said he could not stay in the same room with me, and actually forced the organizers of the meet to give him a private room." The official has never managed a track team outside the country since. Another official Keino could not stand had apparently told lies to meet organizers and fans about how Keino is treated by the government officials back home. Naturally, this hurt Keino's feelings.

Keino disliked cheating, so much so that he might have been one of the very, very few unblemished amateurs before he finally turned pro in 1973. On several occasions he brought back money given to him in meets in the US and

Europe and gave it to the Kenya AAA. As an official of the Nairobi Amateur Athletic Association for two years, 1971-72, I came into contact with every national athlete, and Keino was the rare character who was so honest as to turn down reimbursement for food or transportation if he did not eat on his way to the meet or was given a ride to the meet by a friend.

As the saying goes: "If you try to please everybody, you end up pleasing none." There are those who would find fault with Keino's behavior and the extent of his involvement in helping youngsters or fellow athletes.

The criticism that's received the most publicity is Ben Jipcho's claim that Keino did not thank him after Ben sacrificed his own chances for his countryman in the 1500 at Mexico City. Whether this allegation is true or not, Jipcho's help is certainly acknowledged by Keino in Francis Noronha's biography, *Kipchoge of Kenya*. It is further alleged that Keino participated in the 3000-meter steeple-chase at Munich simply to rob Jipcho of his gold medal. In fact, Keino decided to to compete in the Olympic steeplechase late in 1971 when he realized that in Munich the finals of his favorite events, the 1500 and the 5000 meters, were both on the same day. In May, after a Japanese tour in which Keino clashed with Jipcho in the steeplechase for the first time (Jipcho winning), he told me that he was surprised that the younger athletes he was supposed to be helping to qualify for the Munich Olympics were themselves more interested in beating Keino than meeting the qualifying times.

Although some foreign journalists have said they've found Keino to be somewhat reserved and formal (probably because he's always been careful not to say the wrong thing or to be misinterpreted), Kenyans know him to be very friendly. He has helped many Kenyan youngsters with track shoes and valuable advice (for instance, he gave Mike Boit his first pair of spikes when Mike was in high school). Above all, Keino's exemplary behaviour will be remembered by his countrymen long after his track records are surpassed.

His latest reward from track is a bright future as a businessman. With capital from the ITA, he established a clothing and sports store, and a restaurant at Eldoret. At the time he turned pro, he already had a big tea estate and was part owner (with Charles Mukora) of the profitable Nairobi Olympic Sports House, started in 1969.

He is married with four children, all daughters. The eldest, Emily Jepkoech, was born in December, '63. The third daughter was born to Kip and his wife, Jane, on October 20, 1968—the day he won his Olympic gold medal in Mexico City. They named her, appropriately, Milka Olympia Jelagat.

FILBERT BAYI

Running--"As God Made You."

by Tom Sturak

Tanzania's Filbert Bayi has revolutionized mile/1500-meter running with his ultra-bold pacesetting (a 53-54 second opening 400 is common for him) and his sensational times. His world 1500-meter record of 3:32.2 is equivalent to a 3:49 mile—and Bayi was only 20 when he set that mark! Here is the most complete and incisive story yet written on the Tanzanian super-runner. It was written after Bayi's tour of the US indoor track circuit in early '75. The author, Tom Sturak, is a runner himself and a long-time contributor to Runner's World.

Kip Keino, that most Olympian of African runners, was the first to see the coming glory of Filbert Bayi. The great Kenyan's eyes were opened when the young Tanzanian had rushed away from him to win the African Games 1500 meters on Jan. 13, 1973. The next day, Keino came calling with a prophecy: "If you train hard, you will be the greatest and you will break the world record."

Scarcely more than a year later, at the Commonwealth Games in New Zealand, Bayi did indeed break the world record for 1500 meters in a race that Roger Bannister called "the greatest exhibition of front running that I have ever seen." If not yet the greatest miler of all time, statistically or in honors won, Bayi already must be ranked as one whose genius has changed forever the art of mile/1500-meter running. Like Nurmi and Zatopek before him, he has exercised the will to do astonishing feats that defy commonsense—and thereby has extended the horizons of every runner who aspires to discover his own potential.

Until his 1975 tour of the United States, however, in which he travelled coast-to-coast twice for a series of five races—his first ever indoors—the true dimension of Bayi's genius had only been partially revealed. Known previously as a runner who employed only those "crazy" front-running tactics, Bayi quickly proved himself so bright a student of indoor running and so adaptable that overnight he became a master tactician. Never once did he dash off from the gun a la the Bayi the track world has come to know and marvel at; yet he won every time, running against the likes of John Walker and Rick Wohlhuter, proving he had the speed, strength and acceleration to use whatever tactics he pleased and didn't always have to lead to win.

I spent considerable time with Bayi while he was on the West Coast. I found him to be shy and reserved, often seemingly moody and aloof. By the time we met in Los Angeles (his first race on the tour had been in New York), he had obviously grown weary of running an endless gauntlet of newsmen. However, he allowed me two lengthy interviews; and I was able to observe him up close both at rest and in training over a week's period. I also established a rapport with two of his teammates, Capt. Protase Muchwampaka and Claver Kamanya; and I talked about Bayi with his good friend and chief rival John Walker of New Zealand. In addition, I read everything on Bayi that I could find.

Off the track and on, however, Filbert Bayi has an elusive character. He impresses me as being an extremely intelligent, sensitive, complex and driven young man; but I do not claim to know him.

* * * * * *

Filbert Bayi made his international track debut in the 1972 Olympics in Munich. His only prior serious races had been in the '72 Tanzanian championships a week earlier. Running the 1500 meters and the steeplechase (both for the first time) in the humid heat of Dar es Salaam, he had won both events inside of a half-hour, clocking 3:45.6 and 8:55!

In Munich, however, the unknown and inexperienced Bayi was eliminated in heat one of the Olympic steeplechase, finishing ninth in 8:41.4 (though unrecorded as such, it was the best mark ever by a 19-year-old). A week later, in the second heat of the 1500-meters, he finished sixth in 3:45.4. In both races, he encountered the in-fighting that often mars the high-pressured elimination rounds of the Olympic Games. He was elbowed, shoved and spiked; the experience made an indelible impression on him.

"I might have advanced to the next round in the 1500," he reasoned, "if I had set my own pace, rather than wait and see." Henceforth, he would train so he could lead from gun to tape.

Prior to Munich, Bayi had trained by himself in a rudimentary fashion: "Just running, just for fun on the roads. I was running, crazy, like maybe 12 miles. No track, just roads. I know nothing about track at that time." The roads he ran on were dirt and sand. By "track," he always means interval training—to which he was introduced, at least indirectly, by an East German named Werner Kramer.

Sometime just before the Olympic Games, Kramer had come to assist Erasto Zambi, track coach at the University of Dar es Salaam. After Munich, Zambi (an ex-sprinter), apparently following advice from Kramer, worked out a 100-kilo-meters-a-week training program for Bayi. Included were "sprinting hills twice a week" and "330 intervals on the track."

In the December East African Championships at Dar es Salaam, Bayi ran his third 1500-meters ever in 3:38.2 and almost unnoticed catapulted into the top 10 on the 1972 world list. A month later at the African Games in sweltering Lagos, Nigeria, came his electrifying triumph over Kip Keino. Bayi led the race pole to pole, repulsing Keino in the final 200 meters to win by two seconds in 3:37.2. The sports journalists sat up and took notice.

The intriguing first reports out of Europe quoted the "shy and quiet" Bayi as saying, "If I had been pressed I think I could have run 3:35. And the air was so humid, it was difficult to swallow." Further, Zambi revealed that five days before Lagos Bayi had been "in bed shaken by a malaria attack" with a temperature over 100 degrees. "But under his fragile appearance," Zambi added "he is very tough. Also, we both lack experience and have possibly made many errors in training. I have known him only nine months. He trained by himself before."

Bayi, who pointed out that the Lagos final was only the fifth 1500 of his life, said he wanted to further his running education, so to speak, by racing in Europe and the United States:

"I'm not very fast so I must lead all the time and not pay attention to the other runners. But I would like to have someone set a 3:32-33 pace for 1200

*Filbert Bayi leads into the homestraight in his world record 1500 with (right to
left) John Walker, Ben Jipcho and Rod Dixon in pursuit. (Mark Shearman)*

meters to see what I could do. I have to experiment to understand many things.
Compared to the know-how of the Kenyans, I am ignorant . . . To better my performances, I think I need only to increase the volume of my training and to gain
more experience against the best runners. I'm not afraid of anyone, but I can
learn from everyone."

But as an innocent abroad in the summer of '73, it was Bayi who would
take the best runners to school and show them a new way to race.

On June 28 at the World Games in Helsinki, he scorched the first 100
meters in 12.8, hit the 400-meter mark in 53.6, rushed past 800 and 1200 meters
(with no one close) in 1:51.6 and 2:52.2. Two seconds up on world-record pace,
he at last began to falter; but he pushed on to win in 3:34.6, the third-fastest
clocking ever, equivalent to a 3:51.8 mile. Runners-up Dave Wottle and Ben
Jipcho recorded personal bests of 3:36.2 (3:53.5 mile pace) and 3:36.6 (3:53.9).
Nearly everyone else in the race recorded a personal best, too. Steve Prefontaine ran
3:38.1 (3:55.5) and placed 11th! Twelfth place was 3:38.4 (3:55.8)! A week past
his 20th birthday, only nine months after his first serious competition, Bayi had literally run away from the fastest mass-finish 1500 field in history.

Four days later in a mile at Stockholm, Bayi's pace was even more incredible for the first two 400s: 52.5 and 1:51 flat. Midway through the second lap,
he led Jipcho (and everyone else) by almost 80 meters. He forged on, hitting 1200
meters in an unprecedented 2:52 flat. Though fading, he held the lead through
1500 meters (3:36.4) before succumbing in the final 60 meters to Jipcho,
3:52.6 to 3:52.0. In his first-ever mile, Bayi had become the event's third-fastest
performer in history.

With these two stunning performances, and many others in 1973, Bayi established himself as history's fastest front-runner. Consider the range of his fastest/slowest splits selected from eight major 1500s and the Stockholm mile: 52.5/56.0; 1:51.0/1:54.0; 2:52.0 (twice)/2:53.5. A review of the 10 fastest 1500/mile races before 1973 reveals that in not one of them were the first and second laps faster than 55.9 and 1:54.8, and only a 2:52.5 1200 meters by Jean Wadoux (following pacesetters) en route to a 3:34.0 1500 compares with Bayi's best.

Bayi scored his greatest triumph to date on Feb. 2, 1974, at the British Commonwealth Games in Christchurch, New Zealand, when he broke Jim Ryun's world record for 1500 meters with 3:32.2 (equivalent to 3:49.2 for a mile). During the four days preceding, he had twice lowered his best 800-meter time, placing fourth in the final with 1:45.3, and also posted an effortless 3:38.2 1500 heat.

In the final of the 1500, he led from the start, cruising a relatively slow (for him) 400 of 54.9, but reaching 800 in 1:52.2, and 1200 in an unparalleled 2:50.8. Around the final turn, a trio of fast finishers—Rod Dixon, John Walker, Ben Jipcho—began to sprint. The unheralded Walker drew closest, within three yards, but Bayi simply looked over his shoulder ("to see how fast I had to run") and held his lead to the finish. He ran his final 400 meters in 55.4 (removing some of the doubts people had about his finishing speed). And as in Helsinki barely seven months earlier, his pacesetting had set up another wholesale rewrite of the all-time 1500-meter list: Walker's 3:32.5 moving him to number two on the list; Jipcho's 3:33.2 to number four; Dixon's 3:33.9 to number five; and Australian Graham Crouch's 3:34.2 to number seven.

The following June, Bayi returned to Helsinki—scene of his first great international win the year before—to race 1500 meters. Running faster than ever before, he recorded splits of 52.9, 1:50.4 and 2:50.4. But John Walker, who had trailed by six seconds at 800 meters, sprinted the final 300 in a fast 40.4—while Bayi was struggling through a slow 46.6—to win going away, 3:33.4 to 3:37.0.

Bayi had gone into this race after only five weeks hard training, and he later claimed that he knew he would be beaten: "I knew my shape wasn't good enough to carry that pace all the way through. Actually I was running only a good 1200 meters, like in practice."

Influenced by stories in the press that he would run better off a more sensible early pace, Bayi then began to experiment . . . He won a mile in Stockholm on July 1 in 3:54.1 after running opening laps of 57 and 58. On July 2, he changed tactics even more radically, running in the pack until the final 300 meters and then sprinting to a 3:43.0 win. After that race, however, "he said he felt as tired as if he had run 1:52 instead of 1:57 and that the 'experiment' was over."

But the sportswriters persisted, speculating whether he had found a new way to run—some literally telling him this was *the* way to run the 1500 meters. By July 4 in Oslo, Bayi had decided that the 800 was now his "favorite race," but the meet organizers begged him to run the 1500, "not to disappoint the spectators." He relented but decided again to run "slow, stay with the field and then sprint."

About 950 meters into the race, Mike Boit ran into him from behind: "We both fell," relates Bayi, "and my spikes cut my left knee as I was falling." Result: 12 stitches and a month's layoff. "It was all you journalists' fault!" he told an Italian writer. "If it hadn't been for you, I never would have run that way!"

To this day, Bayi's voice is tinged with bitterness as he tells the story while fingering the U-shaped scar. The incident recharged the resolve made after Munich to run only as he could run best. "Never again in the group!" he vowed after Oslo. "I will train harder so I can start faster and maybe set a 1:49 pace. I am working on it." (And as might be expected, he seems also to have worked on tactics for keeping his distance from journalists.)

Back in Tanzania, Bayi's enforced layoff was extended by a three-month stint in an Army officer's training course. In December 1974, however, after only two weeks of track work, he reluctantly competed in the national championships—mainly to please some "youngsters who wanted to see me running"— winning the 1500 and 800 in slow times. Following a few more weeks of sporadic training, he began the new year, 1975, by returning to Christchurch for the New Zealand Games. He won the 800-meters in 1:45.5, his second-best ever, and ran a 3000-meter time-trial in 7:54.

From New Zealand, Bayi and three other Tanzanian runners, plus a manager, flew to the United States.

* * * * * *

Jan. 30—A day before Bayi's indoor debut in New York, the *New York Times* carries an article on him. Asked if running indoors will cramp his usual fast front-running tactics, Bayi answers: "I don't know myself what it will be like because I have never run indoors, without outside oxygen." The interview, focusing on his East African childhood environment, is charming:

"Sometimes in the morning, you could see Kilimanjaro, before the clouds come," he said. "That was where I learned to enjoy running. Herding my father's cows. Running with my dogs. I am getting stamina all the time. We use the dogs to hunt gazelles . . ."

"How far would you run with them?"

"Depends how soon the gazelle gets tired. Not more than 10 miles."

"When you ran with the dogs after the gazelles, could other boys keep up?"

"Yes, but they didn't have the interest to keep running when they get older. I just love running. It's interesting. It is interest, nothing else . . ."

"Will you become even better?"

"I can break my record," he said quietly. "But another man can break it again."

"Do you think you're the best in the world?"

"I accept what people say," Filbert Bayi said.

* * * * * *

Jan. 31, New York City—Bayi wins the Millrose Games mile, in a meet record 3:59.3. He follows through the first quarter (58.2), then leads the rest of the way (1:58.9, 3:02). "The track was very difficult for me," he says afterwards. "I can't use tactics I use outdoors. That's why I ran in the group." He also says he had trouble breathing the "very dry" air.

* * * * * *

Feb. 7, Los Angeles—Bayi and his teammates are in Los Angeles for the *Los Angeles Times* Indoor Games. I'll meet him for the first time later that evening. Two full hours before his race, in which he will run against John Walker and

Steve Prefontaine, among others, Bayi begins to warm up. He stands out: red flats; green sweat pants with broad, gold stripe; bright red jacket, hood up and tightly tied about the dark fine-boned face. Time after time he flashes by my vantage point, gracefully weaving through the crowded, narrow subterranean corridors of the arena. He stops and does a series of rapidly executed free-form calisthenics. No slow and steady yoga-like stretching; the movements are vigorous, quick. He's super-supple.

I watch the featured mile from trackside by the curve at the top of the back-straight. Obviously not out to run away from the field, Bayi lets Prefontaine take the lead after a lap and is content to float along in second through the half (61.9, 2:02.3). Easing back into the lead, he holds steady to the three-quarter mark (3:02.6), with big, blond John Walker right behind him. The screaming crowd senses a Big Move; and with two laps left, Walker visibly "gathers," moves out a step—but gets nowhere. At each curve, Bayi looks over his shoulder—not throwing desperate glances, but calmly *looking* as a man walking might—and steadily but imperceptibly runs faster. The clock tells you he's accelerating (the final 440 is 57.3) but he shows no evident strain, no dramatic change of form; the stride remains smooth and constant, flowing powerfully from the hips. He finishes fresh in 3:59.3.

"Do you think that maybe Bayi can beat anyone off of any kind of pace?" I ask a well-known track expert afterwards. "Absolutely not. He won't beat Wohlhuter in San Diego. Wohlhuter hasn't lost an important race indoors in years. And Bayi simply doesn't have great acceleration."

Joe Douglas, a former Mihaly Igloi protege, now a successful coach and a close student of middle-distance running, thinks otherwise: "That's absurd! He accelerates, but you don't notice. Bayi is the most efficient runner I have ever seen."

I would add that he is also the most *natural* runner I have ever seen. Most runners are distinguished by personal mannerisms and easily classified by style of stride (e.g., pusher/puller, driver/shuffler). But Bayi simply runs, like water flows or the wind blows.

* * * * * *

Feb. 8, UCLA—It's chilly and threatening rain as the Tanzanians arrive for their workout. They singly go off in different directions to warm up. Bayi pulls the hood over his head and ties the drawstring. We were introduced briefly the night before, but he gives no sign of recognition (possibly because I'm suited up like a dozen others jogging around the Tartan track). So I reintroduce myself. (His handshake, as always, limp and brief. A cultural mannerism?) As he begins to run, I fall in beside and ask how he feels. "Good." I comment that his race last night looked easy. "No race is easy." He obviously does not chat with strangers while running. No matter: after two laps the pace precludes full-sentence utterances from me.

"I'm relieved when all of a sudden Bayi speeds away (it's like watching a receding figure on a speeded-up film), dashes off the track, jumps a low wooden barrier, springs up an aisle to the top of the bleachers, bounds back down the steps, and runs out onto the grass around the first turn. He improvises along this route for two or three miles at a pace I wish I could still race.

Meanwhile, I jog a few laps with Capt. Protase Muchwampaka, an injured hurdler serving as team manager; then a couple miles more with Mwinga Mwan-

jala, a 14-year-old Tanzanian female miler, who speaks little English. "How are you?" I venture. "Fine!" she grins, and then giggles for an entire lap.

Out of sweats and in spikes, Bayi runs four 440s with teammate Suleiman Nyambui (a 13:35 5000-meter runner). Surprisingly, they jog a full lap (sometimes even walking a little) between repeats. On the 440's, Bayi's form is so fluid that it's difficult to guess the pace. Nyambui, a strong and fast runner (1500 meters in 3:39) but not as smooth as Bayi, is a better gauge: he loses ground on the third quarter, and has to rush hard to finish abreast on the last one. (However, he had been so sick with the flu the night before that he had to scratch from the two-mile!)

Capt. Muchwampaka shows me Bayi's times: 57.0, 57.5, 52.2, 54.9. (The plan had been to run between 58 and 62!) Now they're to do 150 meters twice, between 16.5 and 17.6. Striding back up the track, Bayi steps off the distance so he will run toward the finish line. These are apparently all-out efforts, but he manages only 18.1 both times.

The intervals finished, Bayi flops onto the grass and lies on his back, joking with Mwinga Mwanjala, the girl miler, while she pulls off his spikes. Back into sweats, he jogs a few laps to finish up.

* * * * * *

Feb. 9, Inglewood, Calif.—I arrive at the high-rise motor hotel where the Tanzanians are staying. When I had called Bayi earlier to confirm our appointment, he had asked. "How long will be this interview?"

"Maybe an hour."

"Oh, no. One hour, I think that is too many questions."

So we settled on 30 minutes.

Bayi answers the door clad only in blue nylon running shorts. Says he's been trying to sleep, and looks it. He's obviously not in a good mood. The patent cold remedies on the dresser remind me that Nyambui's had the flu. Perhaps Bayi's coming down with it, too.

"Is it still raining?" he asks, pulling open the drapes and staring morosely down on the motel's parking lot whose grimy gray surface matches the sky. He didn't go on the movie-studio tour, because such tours are too long and tiring. He won't run at all today.

To break the ice, I give him a Beverly Hills Striders/Run for Fun T-shirt. He immediately puts it on, checking the fit in a mirror. Though he carries himself well, Bayi is not particularly impressive physically. At 5'10", 135 pounds ("no change since 1972"), he is thin and sleek. Only the long, heavy thigh muscles are well-defined.

He removes the shirt and carefully folds it. "Run for fun," he says softly, almost to himself, with a flickering smile, "Maybe I will run for fun when I am 30." I wonder what it is he runs for now, but file the question away. "Do you plan to compete until you're 30?"

"I don't know." (Three words I'll hear often.)

"Though he carries himself well, Bayi is not particularly impressive physically. At 5'10", 135 pounds ('no changes since 1972'), he is thin and sleek. Only the long, heavy thigh muscles are well-defined." (Mark Shearman)

Setting up the tape recorder, I notice the color TV: the sound is off, but the program appears to be about sharks. Bayi gestures to leave it on. We begin with the basics:

Filbert (he sometimes writes it Philbert) Bayi is his full name. Born June 22, 1953, on a farm near the village of Karatu in the northern area of the Mbulu tribal district, he is the eldest of five brothers and two sisters. His tribe, known by the Swahili name of Wambulu, is commonly called Iraqw; its language, Kiiraqw. He is also fluent in Swahili and English. In 1961, he began attending a government school, and completed seven years. He is Christian (Catholic, his teammates say.) He lived continuously in the Karatu area—at an elevation of about 6000 feet—until the age of 17. In 1970, he travelled the 600 miles to Dar es Salaam, the port-city capital of Tanzania, where he entered military service and has since resided. Trained as an air transport technician, he is now lieutenant with administrative duties. At present a bachelor, Bayi apparently plans to be married soon.

In a later conversation with Protase Muchwampaka and Claver Kamanya, I'm told that the people of Bayi's tribe are well-known for their running abilities. Long distance runner John Stephen—28:44 10,000 and 2:15 marathon in the 1970 Commonwealth Games—also comes from "the same tribe" (it was never made clear to me whether the Iraqw specifically or the Mbulu tribal district generally.) Muchwampaka says that several young runners from "that tribe" are now in training for the Olympic Games. These people, he emphasizes, "have that good early initial training in their lives—walking and running maybe eight miles or more every day while herding, going to and from school, hunting." Kamanya says that although his own background in western Tanganyika was similar, Bayi's boyhood environment was "much harder."

Ninety-six percent of the Tanzanian population—whose citizens are among the poorest in Africa—live on farms. Much of the Tanganyikan hinterland is barely habitable, dependent on capricious rainfall and infested by tsetse fly.

The Iraqw, one of the smaller of Tanzania's 126 tribes (which together total 13 million people), have in the past generation rapidly expanded northward from their traditional homelands "around Kainam, the green, hollowed core of the central highlands of Mbulu, a high, undulating plateau over the rift wall from the Masai." This large plateau ranges in elevation from 4500 to over 6000 feet. (Dr. Roger Bannister, who has done much sports-medicine research, notes Bayi's "built-in altitude acclimatization, inbred over many generations." Bayi himself, however, who has lived at sea level since 1970, claims that "if I go to race at altitude, I will get in trouble, too, because it is too high.")

The Iraqw tribe practices a mixed agriculture and pastoral economy, but practically no homestead is without cattle. Agriculture forms the basis of the subsistence economy—a family cultivating a few acres near its mud-covered thatched hut to grow the corn, millet, sorghum, beans and vegetables that provide the daily diet which is deficient in protein). But the people focus their main interest on the cattle, which are a sign of wealth and social status.

Linguistically, the Iraqw are often classified as Cushitic speakers. The nearest peoples speaking languages of this group live in northern Kenya and Ethiopia. Some linguists, however, are unable to see any connection between Kiiraqw, the language of the Iraqw, and these northern Cushitic languages. Also questionable is the generalization that connections exist between language families and physical characteristics (e.g., that Cushitic speakers show "strong Caucasoid traits", or, as diffused in the track press, that Bayi perhaps has "strong ethnic and linguistic ties" with, say, Keino and Yifter).

Bayi fits well the only psyco-somatotypic description that I found of the Iraqw: " . . . a proud, reserved people, noted for a statuesque, immobile posture and sharply defined features. They tend to be withdrawn."

At the time of Bayi's birth, the extensive tribal district of Mbulu, lying between the Serengeti Plain and the Masai Steppe, was part of the British East African colony of Tanganyika. The region, noted for its abundance and variety of animal life, serves as the setting for several of Ernest Hemingway's short stories. On a clear day, the snows of Kilimanjaro—158 miles (Bayi is precise with numbers) to the northeast near the border of Kenya—can be seen from Karatu.

"When did you start to run?" I ask Bayi. "How did your interest in running grow?"

"Myself, I don't know. That's the question what everybody ask me, but I don't know. You can't know what you will do when you are children. We were running, just running, because at that time nobody knows about running. We were just running: to go into the village, to herd the cows; but you cannot call that running because there is nobody that knows about running first. It is just like walking, as God made you."

"Then, it was just something natural in your daily life?"

"Natural, yes. Because *running* needs training, and at that time I was not training, you see."

"Then you walked and ran everywhere in your everyday life? Were there any cars or bicycles or . . .?"

"No cars or anything like that. Just walking and running."

Bayi is obviously more than a little bored with this line of questioning. He also seems genuinely perplexed that I (like others before me, no doubt) am impressed by his answers. I feel compelled to point out that in the United States most children don't grow up having to walk and run many miles every day; and that when a young man or woman here does run this far every day, it's because he or she wants to be an athlete, not just wants to get from place to place . . .

He nods and murmurs, "I see," and looks out the window. I realize that when I asked him when he started to run I might as well have asked him when he first began to breathe.

"Where and when was your first competition of any kind?"

"I can't remember, because I know we have local competitions all the time; many, many local competitions. But I was about 10. I was jumping, not running."

"Were you good? Did you win?"

"Sometimes somebody beat me. I did about 18 feet (long jump) and 5 feet, 6 inches (high jump)."

"When was your first local running competition?"

"When I was 15, at 5000—but then they call it three miles."

"Did you win that?"

"No, they beat me."

"Were there local coaches or anyone who encouraged you to train?"

"No. But every year we had national championships, school championships, when we competed. At that time, you know, we had some Tanzanian runners. And Kip Keino, I heard about him when I was 16 years. Then I am interested. Then I started running, training.

"So you were inspired by Keino's performances . . ."

"Keino's and Tanzanians', too, because, you know, we had John Stephen and Claver Kamanya and some others who had been running some years ago."

"Did you win a school championship?"

"I was second in 880—in 1969, I think."

"Then these were races on the track?"

"Yes, but we ran barefoot."

"Now in 1970, when you went to Dar es Salaam, did you begin to compete seriously?"

"No; I met some other athletes and began to train casually. But that year I did not start running, because I went there for a [technician's] course. No competition, no training. Just in the morning—there is nobody knowing—I mean, nobody know about me. In '71 , I just tried to train, just slowly on the roads."

"Then, when was your first serious competition?"

"When I compete in the national championships in 1972, a week before Munich."

Of course, I'm astounded (who wouldn't be?). A first-ever 1500 in 3:45 (Bayi's time in the '72 Tanzanian championships) off casual road work! Then I begin to better understand the many apparent contradictions, misinterpretations and errors in published reports of Bayi's training and racing history (and probably that of many other African athletes). In Bayi's case, his English vocabulary is understandably limited, and certain frequently used words become equivocal. For example, *training* and *track* can take on very specific meanings (i.e., programmed intervals, usually sprints), while *running* can be "just running" (as in morning workouts or warmups) or everday "running" ("as God made you") or sometimes stressed "running" (i.e., racing).

"Does Werner Kramer still advise you?" I continue.

"No, he went back to East Germay last year after the Commonwealth Games. But I still follow a program like he gave me after Lagos, put on paper by Zambi, who is the national coach."

"Did Kramer ever advise you about tactics? Did he ever suggest that perhaps you shouldn't go out so fast?"

"No, he said . . . Look, I studied at that time about other runners, in books and magazines, about their strides [pacing?]—for example, Putteman's stride. But Kramer, he tell me, "Your stride is good, too; you run your own way.""

"What do you do for morning workout?"

"Cross-country—six, seven, eight miles."

"Easy pace?"

"Depends, the speed. Sometimes constant speed—three-quarters, 60%."

"I noticed, you don't really jog when warming up."

"Yeah, you know, it depends on what kind of stamina I have. It is the usual thing for me to run like that because I want to use the air [breath deeply? Anaerobically?] I don't like my body to be cold. I want to run continuously."

"Friday night at the arena, you warmed up for about two hours." Why so much?"

"Because there, indoors, the air was cold. I have to warm up two hours— one-and-one-half hour moving, then half-hour jogging. But where it is hot, like in Dar es Salaam, then I need only one hour warmup."

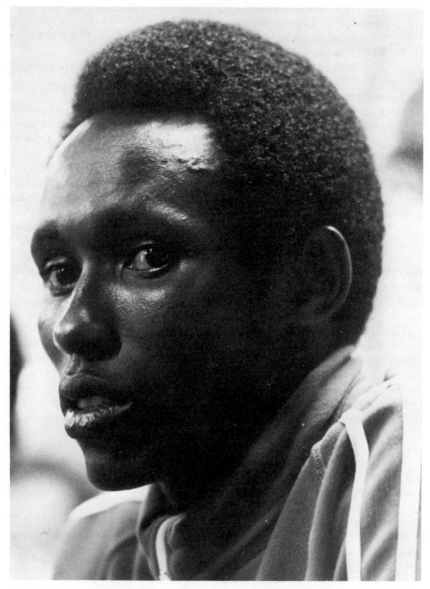

"Like Nurmi and Zatopek before him, he has exercised the will to do astonishing feats that defy commonsense—and thereby has extended the horizons of every runner who aspires to discover his own potential." (Mark Shearman)

"In the afternoons, how do you train typically? About how many miles?"

"Track and speed work. There is no 'How many miles?' for speed work. I keep the record, but it is sprints—you know: 300 meters times four, like that."

"Yes, I saw yesterday at UCLA. But do you ever do more than that, like, say, 20 times 200 or 10 times 400?"

"No, I never need that. That's too much. Because I know how I feel."

"What's the most repeats you ever do?"

"Two-hundred meters time six, 300 meters times six, 500 meters times six, like that."

"All of those in one workout?"

"No, just maybe 300 times six and then maybe 100 or 150 times two or three. But times in training is important. For example, if they told me to run 200 meters times six, it is always almost 25 to 28. But if I'm going to make 30, I'm going to be unhappy. Like yesterday, we planned 58 to 62, but we run 52, 54, 55 . . ."

"So yesterday you ran too fast. Does that bother you?"

"No. But if I ran 62, 64, then it bother me. You know, yesterday, when we ran 150 meters, we planned to run from 16 to 17.2; but we ran 18. We were disappointed with that time, you see."

We're interrupted by a knock on the door. Bayi answers and returns, shaking his head in weary resignation, followed by a man carrying an attache case.

I introduce myself. The man is from *Time* magazine (he says *"Time"* loud and clear); and settles down on the couch. As I continue my interview, I notice that *Time*-man's begun to take notes. I don't like that. When Bayi's telling me about the Oslo race, *Time*-man fairly shrieks: "You were *spiked!*" The expression that passes across Bayi's face like a shadow says it all about journalists. I feel my time is up, but I hold my ground a few minutes longer.

"After the Oslo race, you told an Italian journalist that you were working on a 1:49 opening pace. Are you?"

Bayi answers (shaking his head from side to side): "If it comes, it comes. I am just training to be front runner. In local competitions, I am running in groups. Even now, when I am going to Europe, I am not going to run very fast, even for the first laps. I am training for Olympic Games. I am not training for European tour, American tour."

"Whom do you consider your toughest rivals, the men to beat in Montreal?"

"I fear no man. I mean, as for Montreal, if the Olympic Games were right now, Walker, Wohlhuter would be strong—and many others. But there could be others no one is knowing about."

"Like yourself only a year or so ago . . ."

He does not respond to that. I say my thanks and make sure to add that I'll be seeing him again in San Diego. *Time*-man looks at Bayi and says something like, "Oh, you're going to San Diego? They have a wonderful zoo there . . . "

* * * * * *

Feb. 14, San Diego, Calif.—Nyambui ushers me into the motel room. Bayi's in bed, wrapped as if hiding. He looks less than thrilled to see me; but maybe it's just that he's been sleeping. I ask if he's found San Diego more to his liking than LA. He answers that he hasn't seen much besides this motel and a track.

"You mean no one's even taken you to the zoo?"

"Zoo! Why do we want to go to a zoo? We have a country filled with those animals!"

The color TV is on but mute, and rock 'n' roll blasts from a borrowed stereo. The pile of records and scattered cassettes are Bayi's—brought from Tanzania. (He seems to prefer individual artists—Ray Charles, James Brown, *et al.*—to groups.) Nyambui breaks into a little dance. Bayi's up now, peering into a mirror and teasing his hair with an iron-pronged comb.

Muchwampaka comes in and tells them to suit up for workout. I've volunteered to drive them in my van out to San Diego State University.

By the time we reach the track, the weather's turned cold and the sky's heavily overcast. As usual, Bayi's bundled in his hooded jacket.

His program today calls for six times 150 meters between 16.5 and 17.8, then a 600 in 88 to 90 seconds. I time and Muchwampaka records. Bayi's sprints range between 17.6 (the fourth one) to 16.4 (the second). He's working on these, really digging in over the last 50 yards of each. (Meanwhile, Nyambui's supposed to be running four 500s and four 300s at about 60-second-per-quarter pace. But Muchwampaka keeps chiding him: "Too slow, *bwana!*" On his 600, Bayi looks like he's running in slow motion, flowing through 200 splits of 31, 30, 28.4.

As at UCLA a week ago, the workout transforms Bayi. I had noticed that as as we approached the track, his usual passive, vaguely melancholy expression melted into a look of mellow anticipation. Changing into spikes, he became talkative and all smiles. When he runs, Bayi lights up. In the afterglow, he's friendly, playful, open.

Earl Robinson, a black 4:09 freshman miler at San Diego State, only a few months younger than Bayi, walks right up: "Man, what did it *feel* like in New Zealand when you broke the world record and beat Walker?"

Bayi laughs. "I feel *good!* Walker, he fell down on the track (after the race), but I just kept running around."

Walking back to the van, Bayi puts his hand on Minga's head, giving it an affectionate shake, and remarks that his 14-year-old brother is about the same size. (No, he's not yet a runner.) Then suddenly, he spurts off and goes through a triple-jump routine, which elicits a guffaw and a few pointers from Capt. Muchwampaka.

Back at the motel, Muchwampaka allows me to look at the handwritten interval training program prepared by Erasto Zambi for Bayi and the other three runners on this tour. Later, joined by Nyambui and Kamanya, we chat about Bayi (who even among his teammates seems to be a loner) and about training. Kamanya, at 26, is the oldest and most experienced of the four touring runners. A 45.7 400-meter semi-finalist in the 1968 Olympics, he hopes to run 800 meters at Montreal. He obviously has great affection for Bayi and stands in awe of his stamina ("greater than Keino's"). Kamanya is convinced that Bayi could right now beat any 5000-meter specialist in the world. "His pace is so constant, his stamina so great. I tell you, he is *strong!*"

In the last few weeks prior to the Commonwealth Games, Bayi trained with him "on a 400-meters program," Kamanya says, "repeat 200s in 22-23, 300s in 34-36." Kamanya, who ran 46.2 for third in the Commonwealth Games, believes that if Bayi trained for 400 meters, he could run at least 46.5.

"Bayi is determined and dedicated," Kamanya emphasizes, "even more so than Keino." He recalls that when he and Keino shared a room on a tour, that sometimes they would both sleep in. "But Bayi, he never misses the morning run."

I comment that Zambi's interval program is quite moderate, and ask if perhaps back home in between tours Bayi does harder workouts. Muchwampaka defends the present program as being "very hard work." When I say that many American milers regularly do much more—90 to 100 miles a week, including sessions like 10 times 440 or 20 times 220—the three Tanzanians appear momentarily stunned and then begin to laugh uproariously.

"Why would anyone do such workouts!" Muchwampaka exclaims. "You would be too tired to race!"

Kamanya has literally fallen down laughing, and is barely able to say that in New Zealand John Walker told them that he, too, "sometimes runs 100 miles a week . . ." He can't go on for laughing.

* * * * * *

Feb. 15, 9:30 a.m., San Diego—Bayi breezes in 30 minutes late for our interview (he's been at breakfast) and tells me that someone's coming soon to take him to the San Diego Sports Arena so he can try out the track.

"Haven't you run yet this morning?"

"Yeah, sure, but just running, like warmup."

"I read somewhere that after you beat Keino in Lagos, he advised you to increase your training—that 15 kilometers a day wasn't enough—and that Zambi said then that you would have to run 160 kilometers a week. But from what I've seen, you maybe do 20 kilometers a day at most."

"No. I think maybe 15 kilometers—but maybe not so much even as that."

"You are often quoted as saying that you have no coach, that only you know what to do. But you followed Kramer's program, and one prepared by Zambi for this tour . . ."

"Zambi is only national coach, not my personal coach. Only I know how I feel, you see, how tired I am. If I am tired, I can change the program. Even in the middle, I can change."

"What's the hardest workout you've ever done? So that you are exhausted at the end?"

"There is no workout I do not feel good after it. Look, I never run so fast I am tired, too tired."

I ask if he changes his training before major races or tours by increasing the quantity or quality of intervals. No, he says, the training is always more or less the same. (But he's glancing at his watch, as if in a hurry to get this over with, and I take this answer with a grain of salt.)

Regarding breaks in training, he says that he takes no planned rests but that sometimes, of course, he cannot run because of travelling or his work. When he returns to Dar es Salaam now, he will not train for one week. Also, once a year he takes a month's leave and goes home to Karatu, where "he doesn't run at all"— except in the mornings.

"You know," he says, warming to this subject, "before going to New Zealand just now, I said I did not want to go, because I had no training for three months, because I went for [an officer's] training course; but they said go for experience . . ."

"You mean," I interrupt, "you didn't *train*—did no interval work—for three months and then went to New Zealand and ran 1:45.5 for 800 meters!"

"No running, just Army exercises."

"No running? Even in the mornings?"

"Yeah, sure, sometimes in the mornings—but just like for warmup, you know."

Yeah, I know: maybe six, seven, eight miles at five-minute/mile pace over sandy roads . . . It occurs to me in a flash: this man has never for a day in his life been out of shape, because running is "as God made you . . ."

I ask if he's ever been tested by physiologists or sports-medicine people. Yes, in Sweden they ran him on some machine (his gestures say "treadmill"). But he doesn't recall the words and numbers, only that they told him he was the same as Kip Keino and Ron Clarke and that he could probably break the world record for 10,000 meters without special training.

Bayi has never raced farther than a mile since 1972 or 1973 ("I can't remember," he says), when he did a 5000 meters in "14:13 or 14:17, something like that." He plans to run a few 3000-meter races in Europe this year "for stamina," and also his first-ever cross-country competition (in Italy). But he has no thoughts of ever running 10,000 meters or the marathon. Right now, he is thinking only of Montreal, where he plans to double in the 800 and 1500.

Concerning offers to run professionally, he is adament: "I am always being asked, so I must put it in headlines: 'I AM NOT INTERESTED! NEVER! STAY AWAY FROM ME!' I don't like anyone over me, telling me when I can run. Money is like a flower, very pretty today; but after it blooms, it dies."

I suggest that money could buy him a home; or that he could invest or bank it. "No. It is not enough. And when I am old, the promoter won't like me any more, because I cannot run fast. It won't work!"

What then, I ask, are his personal goals or ambitions beyond running? "Now, I can't say. Only my work—my work is very important to me."

"In 1973, a French journalist said you told him that you dreamed of some-day running a 1500 in 54, 1:51, 2:49, 3:31—which doesn't sound like you—but now that you have run nearly as fast . . ."

"No, no," he cuts in (he's been shaking his head), "I never said . . . Look, that pace is that man's idea. How can I say, some day I will run this time or this time . . . I am not a god!"

******

That evening at the San Diego Indoor Games, Bayi stands by the track with Kamanya, talking quietly, watching the early races with that benign, expectant expression he seems to put on with his running clothes. Now and then, when he turns to stare *up*, wonderingly, at 7'2" Wilt Chamberlain (now grand *patrono* of women's track), he looks like a boy. And you remember (wonderingly) that, as Kamanya says, Bayi is still "a very young man."

A while later, Bayi purposefully makes his way up an aisle in the athlete's section to where John Walker sits talking with Rick Wohlhuter. Bayi greets Walker warmly and initiates a brief conversation. This is the only time that I see him go out of his way to speak to anyone. (If he knows who Wohlhuter is, he never lets on.)

About an hour and a half before his race, Bayi begins warming up. As in Los Angeles the week before, the track has been laid over an (ice) hockey rink and he puts up his hood against the chill air. As Bayi smoothly strides by, a runner friend of mine, who happens to be a doctor, laments: "Oh, he toes out! That's not good."

Francie Larrieu heats up the crowd with a world record 4:29 mile, blasting fast opening laps (as she also had the night before in a record 1500 at Toronto). They are calling her "Filberta."

The "Greatest Indoor Mile in History" starring Bayi, Walker and Wohlhuter, is about to begin. All the entrants except Bayi are up on the track, ready for the call to marks, when he rushes out from a corridor onto the infield, still in sweats, clutching his spikes. He sits down and hurriedly pulls on the striped, calf-length socks and then the brand-new Pumas—while his rivals wait. The old psych? Bayi's elusive character makes it difficult to guess.

From the gun the pace is fast, but a runner named Ed Zuck, not Bayi, is responsible. Later it's reported that Bayi was ignorant of the "rabbit" role played by Zuck, who led through blistering splits of 54.5, 1:57.8. I don't for a moment believe it; Bayi may be naive about some things, but not about runners and racing. He was also quoted by *Sports Illustrated* as saying, "I think the guy who kicked from the start, he didn't like to win." But when I talked to Bayi after the race he said that the first 440 was not too fast at all, that he would have liked it faster.

More interesting (if not such "good copy") was the slow third quarter (63.4, Bayi leading), that lost the fans a world record but won him a brilliant tactical battle. Watching Bayi one might have noted nothing more than the fact he often looked behind when coming out of the turns—and that he stayed in front. But what was happening with Wohlhuter told the whole story. Never more than a tick behind through three-quarters, he was the natural favorite—an experienced, proven first-class indoor runner with a long string of victories on the boards. Yet running behind Bayi's varying tempo, Wohlhuter appeared an awkward novice, often left hanging up on a curve, once running into Bayi's spikes, looking more tense and less threatening with every passing lap.

Afterwards, Wohlhuter, visibly dazed, rationalized that he was not used to "running this kind of (slow) tempo . . . I'd get bogged down, start running to catch up, then have to slow again." In other words, Bayi had played with the pace and with him. As Walker (well-versed in Bayi's tactics) explained later: "Bayi runs where he goes fast—he surges the whole way, and slows it down, he surges . . . you've got to run behind him (to know), he surges . . ."

And with one final (barely noticeable) surge, Bayi for the second week in a row eluded the hard-pursuing Walker by a half-second, winning in 3:56.4 (equal third on the all-time indoor list), with a final quarter of 55 flat.

A hard-pursuing clutch of newsmen, however, prove impossible to shake. Holding Filbert at bay in a concrete-walled storeroom that serves as temporary television studio, they grill him as he sits on a low table, his sweat-coated face glistening under the spotlights. Still on a physical "high," he answers in a staccato rhythms and almost-pidgin phrases.

"How did you feel on the last lap?"

"Yeah, the last lap was good. Because you know I was waiting for Wohlhuter and Walker because they were close to me when we had three-quarters laps—when we had only one quarter—but when the gun was shot up for the last lap, I was not strength (running fast?), because there was nobody following me. And when I was at the corner for the last (quarter) I thought I was under world record—that why I had been relaxing through the way—and I was not very tired as I had been in Los Angeles and New York."

"You felt better tonight than you did in those races?"

"Yeah, sure. But, you know, I have some pains here (rubbing his shin)—all of us Tanzanians are hurting in the legs from too-hard tracks we run speed work on here."

"Were you surprised when Wohlhuter did not attempt to take the lead when maybe two laps were remaining?"

"No, I like him to take the lead; but he didn't. I think I like him to lead the way—for the last quarter—him to be close to me, and then we can make the thing, you know." He makes lightly clenched fists and pantomimes boxing. "But I did not know how many feets, I mean, how many meters, he was behind. I didn't look behind."

Receiving the high-sign that's time about up, the television announcer thrusts the silver, golf-ball headed microphone close to Bayi's face and asks the Big One:

"If you ran outdoors right now, what could you run? With a good pace, with Walker?"

Bayi's jaw and mouth set momentarily into a grim mask. He breathes in deeply through his nose, then suddenly grins and looks the man straight in the eyes:

"I don't know . . . I think . . . hmmm" (as in "How 'bout"), "three-forty!"

Pause (you can almost hear the gears grinding): "Oh, 1500 meters?"

"Yeah, yeah, sure," Bayi says slowly, almost inaudibly. He's grown weary of this game.

An AAU official comes up and asks for Bayi's signature on a yellow form that will certify his time as "a new Tanzanian indoor record." The three official watches showed "an unusual spread" (3:56.0, 3:56.4, 3:56.8). Bayi couldn't care less.

"I was not running for a good time, but just to win tonight, because now I've got some experience. Now I learn, I think, 50% of the things that I want to learn. But I need to learn more."

Much later in the night, between parties, I look in on Muchwampaka and Kamanya to say good-bye. Bayi appears (it's the only word, he moves so softly) in our midst, dressed for bed (i.e., blue nylon running shorts). I tell him that I have been talking with John Walker, who had many good things to say about him.

"Yeah," he says very softly, "Walker . . ." Then, in hushed tones, he tells Muchwampaka: "You know what Walker says to me before the race? That in Toronto he goes all night to a party with girls . . ." He shakes his head, smiling— and then is gone.

* * * * * *

Bayi himself says it most succinctly: "Everybody now is training to beat Filbert." He has become the model and measure for all who would race the 1500/ mile. No middle-distance runner of note can escape the question: "If you were up against Bayi in the Olympics, how would you run?"

Marty Liquori says, "Well, I wouldn't go with him. I would just try to key off his pace and run maybe a little faster than I normally do, and then hope to catch him at the end."

John Walker, one of the three men who hold victories over Bayi at 1500 meters since Munich, says, "The main thing when racing against Bayi is making sure that you're with him with 400 meters to go. Because . . . he goes off at such a hurried rate that he gets into oxygen debt and he can't kick home."

Ben Jipcho (now a professional) says that he thinks both John Kipkurgut and Rick Wohlhuter could outkick Bayi.

What it will take, in terms of pace, to beat Bayi at his front-running best outdoors, is scary for all to contemplate. Liquori demurs: "Whether John Walker or Filbert Bayi can run 3:47 (for the mile)—I can't run 3:47 . . . (But) I don't think anybody is going to run the equivalent of 3:47 at the Olympics (due to the pressure in Olympic competition)."

Walker thinks that with "sensible pacing" he (Walker) can run "four 57s" for a mile, and "can go through in 2:50 quite easily and kick home" in 1500 meters. That may or may not be fast enough.

Bayi, in his world-record 1500, sprinted the final 300 in 41.4 off an average pace of 56.9! But he himself has a ready answer for anyone who would ask the inevitable: "If you can tell me the day on which you are going to die, I will tell you when I will run 3:30 for 1500 meters or 3:47 for a mile."